A Mother's
Footprints of Faith

Other Books by Carol Kuykendall

Learning to Let Go
Give Them Wings
What Every Mom Needs (with Elisa Morgan)
What Every Child Needs (with Elisa Morgan)

A Mother's Footprints of Faith

Stories of Hope and Encouragement

Carol Kuykendall

ZondervanPublishingHouse
Grand Rapids, Michigan

A Division of HarperCollinsPublishers

A Mother's Footprints of Faith
Copyright © 1997 by Carol Kuykendall

Requests for information should be addressed to:
⛪ ZondervanPublishingHouse
Grand Rapids, Michigan 49530

Library of Congress Cataloging-in-Publication Data

Kuykendall, Carol, 1945–
    A mother's footprints of faith : stories of hope and encouragement / Carol
Kuykendall.
       p.   cm.
    ISBN: 0-310-21083-6 (hardcover)
    1. Kuykendall, Carol, 1945– . 2. Christian biography—United States. 3. Mothers
—United States—Biography. 4. Spiritual biography—United States. I. Kuykendall,
Carol, 1945– . II. Title.
BR1725.K88A3   1997
248.8'431—dc21   96-51523
                                                        CIP

This edition is printed on acid-free paper and meets the American National Standards
Institute Z39.48 standard.

Published in association with the literary agency of Alive Communications, 1465 Kelley
Johnson Blvd., Suite 320, Colorado Springs, CO 80920

Interior design by Sue Vandenberg Koppenol

Printed in the United States of America

---

97 98 99 00 01 02 03 /❖ DH/ 10 9 8 7 6 5 4 3 2 1

To my daughters Lindsay and Kendall,
and to my friend Dale, a new mother.
To all those coming along behind me,
walking the same path.
May these stories encourage you
and offer hope along the way.

Contents

f i v e
Finding the Way

Acknowledgments

This book grew out of many relationships and sources of encouragement, so I am filled to the brim with "thank you's."

To my husband, Lynn, who believed in me when I didn't believe in myself. And for his patience as I nearly cocooned myself in this project.

To my children, whose lives provided the stage for many of these stories, for their understanding during this book-writing era. During those visits when they briefly returned to the Empty Nest, they endured lots of take-out food.

To my extended family—my sister Joan and brothers Dexter and Mark—for the family threads and loyalty that tie us all together.

To my friends and coworkers at MOPS International, especially Elisa Morgan, Karen Parks, Beth Lagerborg, and Lynne Giddings, who read these stories and made helpful suggestions.

To my faithful prayer-partner friends Joyce Hutchens, Kathy Raybin, Anne Fletemeyer, Carol Dafferner, and Sylvia Free, who have been my cheerleaders in many "fourth quarters."

To editors Sandy Vander Zicht and Rachel Boers at Zondervan for their insights and guidance.

To Rick Christian at Alive Communications for being my advocate.

To all the mothers in MOPS groups everywhere, for your faces and hearts, which became the motivation for my writing.

Foreword

"Wouldn't it be great if we could live life backward?" Carol asked as we walked along a beach at a reservoir in Denver, Colorado.

"Wouldn't it be great if we could live life already knowing all the lessons we learn along the way? Think how much simpler life would be . . ." Carol was finishing up this book and thinking out loud, wheels turning, gears grinding. I listened, as I usually do when Carol talks. "It'd be like—well, like knowing where to put your feet, one step at a time."

We stopped on the shore and stood, side by side, looking back at our footprints—clear marks in the sand behind us. Yes. Life would be soooo much simpler if we could live it backwards. We'd know how to handle the kinds of issues we all face, before we even approached them. Longings. Questions about who we are. How to mother. When to let go. What really matters. Loneliness.

In *A Mother's Footprints of Faith*, Carol takes us along on her life's journey with a collection of personal stories—stories that clearly weave a path through life's many lessons. Her footprints are evenly spaced. They are easy to make out, even around bends and in rocky spots. And they lead faithfully, step by step, closer and closer to the realization that we do not walk alone on the path of life. Rather, God walks beside us.

We can't live life backwards, beginning at the end. But we can live it with a friend who has "been there, done that." And that's the next best thing.

Elisa Morgan
President, MOPS International

Sharing the "Stuff"
of Our Lives

On a sunny Friday morning in early spring, I rang my friend Dale's doorbell and checked my watch. 7:36. Only a few minutes late.

"Come in, come in!" Dale said enthusiastically as she swung open the door.

As I stepped into the living room, my eyes were drawn to the basketball-sized bulge under her oversized shirt. Dale was two weeks from the due date of her first child.

"How's Simon?" I asked, patting her tummy. I'd started talking to her unborn baby, just like she did.

"He's huge. He's got to enter the real world soon," she said, flopping down on the couch. "I can hardly breathe or sleep or put on my shoes."

"I remember the feeling. How can I help?"

In the past year, Dale and I had built a comfortable relationship, ever since we were connected through a mentoring program at our church. The guidelines were simple: *meet together regularly and share your lives.*

Neither of us knew exactly what that meant. We were at opposite ends of one of life's chapters. She perched on the edge of starting her family. I stood ready to exit that place as the last of our three children was graduating from high school. Having been married twenty-eight years, my husband, Lynn, and I were ready to become empty nesters. Dale had just celebrated her sixth anniversary and twenty-ninth birthday; I was turning fifty.

What could I give her? I wondered at the beginning of this relationship. *What is the "stuff" of our lives that we have to share?* Surely, I am no expert. I don't have any guaranteed formulas or easy answers to life's bewildering questions. I am still filled with my own questions and fears of inadequacies, my own growth and transitions into new chapters and challenges.

What could I possibly tell someone just starting out?

FRIDAY MORNINGS

We committed to meet every Friday morning at 7:30 before work, sometimes at my house, sometimes at hers, but usually at a convenient neighborhood coffee shop where I sipped strong coffee and she always ordered herbal tea. Then, for at least an hour, we talked.

As the months passed and our friendship grew, I found that I did have something to share. I had my life experiences, which are remarkably similar to her challenges: trying to understand how her childhood experiences affect the choices she is making as a wife, daughter, and mother; wondering how to parent or balance priorities or resist temptations or find meaning in the mundane routines of her life.

So instead of giving her answers, I told her my stories. Memories of my own confusing longings of adolescence, when I began to yearn for something I didn't have even though I didn't know what I wanted. My surprising transitions to marriage and motherhood, which revealed unknown parts of me to myself. Those fatiguing, pell-mell days when I cared for three children under the age of five, mostly loving the challenge but feeling guilty when I didn't. The unexpected difficulty of the role reversal of caring for my dying mother.

Yet as I recalled these memories, I began to see them differently than when I had lived through them. In looking back at them, I saw their greater meaning and purpose. I saw them with a clearer perspective.

Perspective means to pass beyond something and look back at it and see it in a whole new way. It is a grid through which we sift our memories; a grid that grows out of the passage of time as we mellow and move beyond some of the confusion and intense emotions of the moment; a grid that gives us the ability to see more of life from God's point of view and fit our experiences into his greater picture.

FINGERPRINTS AND FOOTPRINTS

In my Friday morning conversations with Dale, I've discovered the unexpected blessings of seeing my memories in this whole new way—especially those memories of raising young children, when it was all I could do to keep up with the daily tasks of wiping their grimy fingerprints from the countertops and their muddy footprints off the hallway floor. Back then, there seemed precious little time for reflection.

But in looking back, it isn't the dirt or drudgery I see. It is the evidence of God's presence in those experiences. So often, while living in the midst of those hectic days, I didn't even think about God's nearness. So often, in my weariness or frustration, I felt unsure of myself and unaware of God's love.

This is the joy of looking back. I see with greater clarity and can say with stronger conviction that God *does* weave all things together for good in everything. In his time. Just as he promises.

And great good grows out of something else: a pattern of footprints. Not a child's muddy footprints, but my own—footprints that mark significant steps of progress in my journey of faith, places where I reached the limits of my own strength and turned to God. Places where I began to recognize a longing, and that longing drew me closer to him. Places where I began to stand on God's promises.

These are my footprints of faith.

SOMETHING FOR YOU

"What's in this for you, Dale?" I asked as we sat on the couch that Friday morning. She pondered my question as she massaged her bulging stomach.

"Encouragement," she answered simply. "To see more of my daily circumstances from God's point of view. To accept my feelings and put them into perspective. You've gathered more pieces of life's puzzle, so your stories give me hope."

That's my hope as I write down these stories for you.

My stories are not so unusual. Most are descriptions of every-day experiences with the added ingredient of a look back at that experience now. As you read them, I hope you begin to believe that God is present in your life today, even if you don't see him. I hope you trust that our lives are the platforms upon which God's plans are worked out.

Each story highlights a footprint Scripture—a biblical promise that gave me firm footing in a wobbly place and moved me a step closer to God—and several footprint lessons, truths and practical applications gleaned from each experience.

"A Record of Footprints" will give you an opportunity to begin recording some pivotal places in your own memories: reflections from your childhood or last year or even last week; places where life seemed to turn a corner. Through your personal reflections, I hope you will see your own pattern of footprints beginning to emerge, marking those places where you began to recognize and respond to the One who faithfully orchestrates your circumstances as he draws you to himself.

Finally, you will find "A Collection of Promises," some of the timeless biblical truths about what God will do for those who love and trust him. The promises are organized according to your needs:

When you feel all alone . . .

When you are tired and discouraged . . .

When you wonder about your purpose in life . . .

Maybe in this collection, you will find the promise you need to stand on today.

Becoming a mother forever changes the way we look at the world; the way we look back and review our own childhood and fam-ily relationships. Whether you are a new mom or an experienced one, my hope as you read this book is that the following pages will take you beyond my life's lessons to begin thinking about your own stories . . . and your own footprints of faith.

part one

Experiencing Longings

He has also set eternity in the hearts of men.
Ecclesiastes 3:11

Something wondrous happens when a woman becomes a mom.

Suddenly she begins to look at all of life a bit differently. She finds herself in the middle of two generations and sees both in a whole new light. She watches her children respond to life and experiences a renewed sense of childlikeness.

She thinks about her own childhood.

She also looks at her parents, especially her mother, in a new way. She considers the ways in which she was parented and she understands. She thinks about sibling relationships—her own and those of her children.

Often these thoughts reawaken some longings she experienced in her childhood.

Through time she learns that God creates longings in our hearts in order to draw us closer to him.

one

I Wanna' Be a Cheerleader!

My mother always promised . . .

In high school, I wanted to be a cheerleader.

That may sound like a silly goal, but when I went to high school, girls didn't have competitive sports programs. If we were athletic, cheerleading is about all we had. Besides, the popular girls were cheerleaders. I wanted to be popular. So naturally, I wanted to be a cheerleader.

Sounded logical to me. Attainable too, because my mother raised me with her favorite promise in my heart: *You can do anything you want to do and be anything you want to be . . . as long as you just try hard enough.*

I believed her, and carried that confidence into my sophomore year.

I attended a brand-new high school where cheerleader tryouts were open to everyone. Several of my friends decided to try out, and we all began practicing together in the auditorium after school. I also practiced at home in our driveway, in the bathroom in front of the mirror, and alone in my bedroom. I even practiced in my sleep as I dreamed about becoming a cheerleader. I got those routines down and those kicks up. By the time those cheerleader tryouts rolled around, I had practiced as long and hard as anyone else I knew.

So I marched out in front of that all-school assembly in the auditorium, feeling jittery but also excited, because I was prepared. I performed my individual routine perfectly. I even threw in a couple of extra kicks. I did the group cheers with my friends. Then we all ran out of the auditorium while the students voted. Everyone went back to class, and we began to wait for the results.

To this day I can distinctly remember the sound of the PA system as it crackled and then clicked on toward the end of eighth period algebra class that afternoon.

I heard the principal clear his throat, and my hands turned clammy cold.

"Attention, students!" he said with enthusiasm. "I have the results of the cheerleading election here, and I will read the six names in alphabetical order."

I kept my head down, as if studying my paper, but I didn't see a thing on the page. My heart pounded so loudly I was certain those around me could hear it.

He started through the list. One name . . . two names . . . three . . . and on. Since my last name started with a "V" for Van Ark, I held out hope, but he got to the sixth and last name somewhere in the S's . . . and slowly I began to realize I had not been selected.

Somehow I got through the rest of that class. Finally the bell rang, and I tried hard to fix my face so that I could march down that crowded hallway, looking as if the loss hardly mattered to me. I knew I had to get to my locker and tell my friends who had made it that I was happy for them. I had to keep smiling and pray that I could hold the tears inside of me until I got home.

It was awful, but I did get through it, and that night, as I lay on my bed feeling the agony of failure, I thought about my mother's promise. She was wrong. I couldn't be anything I wanted to be. I couldn't do anything I wanted to do merely by trying hard enough.

It was a moment of great pain and confusion.

As I look back on that experience, I still remember the pain, but I also see it as a pivotal point of positive change and growth in my life. For most of my childhood, I blindly believed what my mother told me. But the day when I lost that cheerleading election, I realized she was wrong.

It wasn't my mother's fault, of course. Now that I am a mother, I understand mothers better. I know we do the best we can, and we don't always realize how our children put their faith in what we say and sometimes take our words of encouragement as promises.

But in the growing-up process, a child reaches a major turning point when she realizes her mother is not always right and her promises are not always true.

For me, that realization led to a puzzling question: *If I can't count on my mother, who or what can I count on?* That's an important question to ask when you're growing up. And the answer makes a big difference in the way you live the rest of your life.

I spent many quiet hours sitting alone in my bedroom during that sophomore year pondering the answer to that question. I felt all mixed-up with a yearning in my heart, but for what, I didn't know. Yet in the midst of that insecurity, I kept looking out of my window at the majestic Rocky Mountains across the valley from our house. Sometimes I picked up the Bible an aunt had given me, and I read the words of Psalm 121:

> *I lift up my eyes to the hills—*
> *where does my help come from?*
> *My help comes from the LORD,*
> *the Maker of heaven and earth.*

The Psalm included some other promises:

> *He will not let your foot slip . . .*
> *The LORD watches over you . . .*
> *The LORD will keep you from all harm . . .*

I loved my mother and wanted to believe her promise. I wanted life to be fair and predictable. I wanted to believe I could *be anything I wanted to be and do anything I wanted to do* simply because I tried hard enough. I wanted to control the results of my efforts simply by the depth of my longing and determination. But when I lost that cheerleading election, I began to see that sometimes the world created barriers that I couldn't overcome. Sometimes my dreams wouldn't come true no matter how hard I tried.

In facing that reality, God began to kindle a yearning within me for himself, and I began to find strength in the words of those promises in Psalm 121. I knew that even when my life in high school seemed filled with unpredictable circumstances, God was like those rock-solid mountains he created outside my window: always present and never changing. And when I ran smack dab into a barrier like this one, God was there watching over me, assuring me he had something better in mind.

Only in looking back do I see the significance of that pivotal event. When I hit that barrier, I turned toward God and started trusting his promises. I started opening my eyes and looking for that something else that he had in mind for me. I started believing that something else would be better for the person he was growing and shaping me to be.

That year, I turned away from cheerleading and toward creative writing, the school newspaper, and journalism. It was an interest that clicked for me. I eventually became the editor of the school newspaper and went on to major in journalism in college.

In looking back, I see how that cheerleading loss helped change the direction of my life. I hit a barrier, turned a corner, and came face-to-face with God, who promised that he was watching over me, that he had a better plan, and that he would guide my steps.

And I started believing him.

Footprint Scripture

The promises of the LORD are promises that are pure, silver refined in a furnace on the ground (Ps. 12:6 RSV).

Footprint Lessons

- In growing up, we reach a moment when we realize our parents are not always right. This is not their fault. Only God is always right.

- A longing for truth is a longing for God. His promises are always true.

- When we hit one of life's barriers, perhaps God wants us to change direction. He may have something better for us right around the next corner.

Reflections

1. Describe a moment when you realized your mother or father might not be right all the time. How do you view that experience today? Do you see it as a step of personal growth? Explain.

2. Describe a time when you lost something you really wanted, such as a job or an election or position on a team. Is it because you didn't try hard enough? Explain.

   What did you learn from that experience?

3. How has God used that loss (or any other losses or failures) to shape you into the person you are today? How has your redirection brought you something better?

4. What kind of a barrier have you encountered that turned you toward God?

two

Me and My Daddy

I longed for a closer relationship

I always longed for a perfect daddy. Or at least a perfectly good relationship with my imperfect father. I got neither. And I'll never forget the day I lost my chance to try.

It was mid-September, a few years after my husband Lynn and I were married. Derek, our first child, had just turned a year old, and I'd recently learned I was pregnant again. Lynn was in the Navy and we lived in San Diego, far away from home in Colorado. Though my father had cancer and I knew he was dying, I still felt shocked when the phone call jarred us awake a little before six that morning.

"Honey," my mother said quietly. "It's over."

We immediately made plans to fly home.

I got Derek up and started to feed him while Lynn placed some phone calls.

"Carol's father died this morning," I heard him tell someone as I poured some juice into Derek's cup. Suddenly the reality of those words began to sink into me. The reality that I'd lost not only my father, but the opportunity to build a better relationship with him. I'd lost my chance to replace some difficult old memories with some good new ones.

A few hours later we were sitting on an airplane, zooming toward home in Colorado. Derek had fallen asleep in my lap, and I looked out the window at the clouds in the sky and began to sort through a confusing jumble of memories about my father. He was a man with fierce family loyalty, but also a fierce temper that had always frightened me.

"He's a Dutchman," my mother used to say, rationalizing his temper as if it were something he was born with, like blue eyes, so he couldn't help it. At times he seemed especially caring and sensitive, but at other times he would blow up like a volcano. Though the eruptions didn't last long, I felt wounded by the hot lava. I hated the unpredictability of his temper.

During the week of the funeral, my two brothers and sister and I had plenty of time to talk about our memories, and naturally, we all chose to remember the good ones. The way he always made sure we had enough change in our pockets when we went out "just in case you need to call home." The way he wrote us one-line notes of encouragement and left them on a bureau or the kitchen counter, which helped us realize that he expressed himself better in writing than in speaking.

"Carol, do you remember how he talked you into becoming an accordion player?" my younger brother Mark asked. We all laughed, recalling the details.

It was the summer I turned eleven, an awkward, in-between time in my life. I was too old to play with toys and too young to wander around the shopping mall with my friends. So I moped around the house, sometimes making big batches of chocolate chip cookies and eating globs of the dough, mostly out of sheer boredom.

No wonder I chubbed up that summer.

To make matters worse, I started needing glasses and chose an absolutely hideous pair that had navy blue frames with rhinestones in the pointy corners. They never fit right and kept slipping down my nose.

One night I overheard my mother talking to my father about me.

"She's looking for herself," she said.

I didn't know what that meant, and I doubted that my father even heard her.

"Hmmmm," is all he said.

The very next evening I sat down next to him on the porch after dinner. Somewhere in the background a radio played accordion music.

"How would you like to play the accordion, Carol?" he asked me, right out of the clear blue. "I'll bet you'd be invited to lots of parties, because people would want you to bring your accordion and play for them."

"Wow, that sounds swell," I said, thinking about all those parties as I looked up at my father and pushed my glasses up on my nose.

The next Saturday, my father took me to a store where parents rent musical instruments for their children until they see whether a whim turns into a genuine commitment. The moment we walked into the store, I spotted the accordion of my new dreams. It was gaudy gold and sparkly, and while my father talked to a salesperson, I pulled the heavy thing on, clumsily straddled a stool, and began pushing the left-hand buttons, which produced wonderfully eerie church organ sounds.

Instantly, I knew I'd found myself.

Soon my father made arrangements to rent the instrument, and I walked out of the store wearing my accordion like a new pair of shoes.

When I got home, my brothers and sister begged to play it, but my father stopped them.

"This accordion is not a toy," he told them gruffly. "It's Carol's musical instrument."

I puffed right up with importance. A few weeks later he found me a teacher, and every Thursday night he would come home from work, gulp down a quick dinner, and drive me to my lesson. He would carry the heavy case into the teacher's studio and then sit in the car, reading the newspaper in the dim evening light. Meanwhile, I learned to play the "Liechtensteiner Polka" and "Lady of Spain." I'm sure I was a sight . . . a chubby girl with glasses pumping away on that gaudy gold accordion.

The next summer I turned twelve, and my father surprised me on my birthday by telling me he had purchased the accordion. Wow, now I could be an accordion player for life!

But the euphoria didn't last. That fall I entered junior high school and slowly new friends and phone calls and Friday night slumber parties became more important than playing the accordion. Especially since my new friends teased me about it.

"*Nobody* plays the accordion," they said. And you can bet I didn't want to be a *nobody!* So I practiced less and found excuses not to go to lessons.

"What's the matter, Carol?" my father asked one Saturday morning when I returned from a slumber party. "Don't you like the accordion anymore?"

I kind of shrugged my shoulders and went down the hall to my room.

Soon after that I stopped taking lessons, and in a response totally unlike my father, he didn't get mad at me about it. The accordion was simply stored in a closet way back under the stairs and no one ever mentioned it.

"Your accordion is still there," my brother said as we all sat around the dining room table that day. "I came across it yesterday when I was sorting through some stuff."

The next afternoon we buried my father, and before I knew it, Lynn and I were back on the plane to California. As I looked out that window at the clouds once more, I again thought about my father and some of those difficult memories: the painful misunderstandings between us; his unpredictable angry outbursts; my longing to feel close to him. I felt a sense of great emptiness and grief. *What would I do with these longings?*

For several years after that, my longing and grief grew more intense, especially when I saw a father tenderly hug his daughter or heard a friend talk about her "awesome" relationship with her dad. As our own family grew, I learned more about family dynamics and dysfunctional relationships.

Did I have a dysfunctional relationship with my father? I wondered.

Suddenly one day I found an answer to that question, which also helped me see my relationship with my father in a whole new way. While attending church one day, I heard a summary statement about the Bible that changed my perspective: *The whole Bible is the story of a dysfunctional family—and their redemption.*

That single sentence helped me realize that lots of people have dysfunctional relationships in their families. It means we don't function together exactly right. But God makes a promise that for all who receive him, he gives the right to become children of God. That means if I believe in God, I become part of God's family, and as a child in that family, I inherit a whole new way to look at all the other relationships in my life. I don't have to see them the way I used to or get stuck in any of their malfunctions.

I know that my father and I didn't always function well together, even though we had some good times. My father was not perfect, and he did have a temper. But I'm not perfect either, and God forgives me for that. So I can forgive my father.

I also realized that I have a choice about all those stored-up memories. I have some control over which ones I pull out and rerun across the screen of my mind. And even if I bring out some of the difficult ones, I don't have to respond to them with the same feelings I had when I was six. Or ten. Or sixteen. I can respond to them with the understanding I have now. I can also choose to rerun more of the good ones, like the accordion memory.

As for my unfulfilled longing to have a closer relationship with my father, I realize that God creates this instinctive "father-hunger" in the heart of every child for a purpose. My father satisfied a small portion of that hunger, and for that I am thankful. Through the remaining emptiness, the unmet emotional needs and longings, God continually enlarged my longing for him. He turned my hunger and searching into a yearning for one who loves me unconditionally, who is sufficient to meet all my needs and longings, and who never changes.

He is my heavenly Father.

Footprint Scripture

Yet to all who received him, to those who believed in his name, he gave the right to become children of God (John 1:12).

Footprint Lessons

- God creates an instinctive "father-hunger" in the heart of every child that draws us to our heavenly Father.

- As children of God, we inherit a whole new way to view our family relationships.

- No one has a perfect relationship with a father or mother, because we all are imperfect people. And because of our own imperfections, we can forgive our parents for being imperfect.

- Our minds are filled with memories of the past. We have choices about which memories we pull out and rerun across the screens of our minds.

- Our longing for a closer relationship with a father is a longing for God.

Reflections

1. How did becoming a parent change the way you view your relationship with your own parents?

2. We choose which memories we keep rerunning across the screen of our minds. What is a favorite memory of your father? Your mother?

3. How do you want to parent your children differently from the way you were parented?

4. If you have a difficult memory of your relationship with either parent, how might God use that experience to draw you closer to him?

5. What does it mean to you to be a "child of God" (John 1:12)?

three

Going Home

Why can't everything stay the same?

The Christmas after my father died, I came home to Colorado anxious for assurance that nothing had changed. I wanted to know that the holes created by my father's absence would not alter our family. I longed for the comfort and security of finding the same, predictable Christmas traditions in spite of this major difference.

I didn't know how unrealistic that was until I arrived at my mother's house with my husband, Lynn, and one-year-old son, Derek. The minute I stepped into the front hall, I knew things were never going to be the same.

I also began to fear that my mother had lost it. Totally.

I knew she had rented out the basement level of our two-story home to a young couple. We all thought that seemed wise. The downstairs had its own outside entrance; she didn't need all the space, could use the extra money, and wouldn't be living all alone in that big house.

I also knew that during our visit Lynn and Derek and I would be squeezing into a small room off the garage instead of having the downstairs to ourselves. That would be fine too.

But I wasn't prepared for the way in which my normally organized mother had dealt with a bunch of leftover stuff she couldn't quite sort through as she downsized her living space and adjusted to life without my father. She merely piled it all haphazardly into the stairwell that wound downstairs, right off the front hall. Then she covered the pile with a festive, bright red blanket, and finally, as if to add a touch of humor to the whole mess, she named the area. On a piece of cardboard taped to the mirror above the stairwell, she had written the words "The Mine Shaft" in black crayon, with a big black arrow pointing down.

I didn't think it was funny.

Did this mark the beginning of the weird way my mother dealt with grief and loss?

Did it mean she was turning into one of those eccentric older ladies who saved everything, including stacks of old newspapers and sacks of junk until they piled up to the ceiling, leaving only a few square feet of living space?

"Mother, what is this mess?" I asked incredulously as I dropped my suitcase and pointed to the junk in the stairwell.

She laughed.

"I didn't know where to put it and that seemed like a perfect temporary solution under the circumstances."

I liked the word "temporary;" I didn't like the phrase "under the circumstances."

As that Christmas unfolded, several other changes became evident. Most were more subtle than The Mine Shaft. For instance, my family always took pride in finding a perfectly shaped tree that just touched the ceiling in our living room. My father sometimes waited at a local tree lot until a fresh load came in, and then picked the best one right off the truck.

This year, the tree in the living room was about half the size and woefully misshapen.

"I thought it had personality," my mother said simply.

I had to admit that, in trees, I liked perfection better than personality.

Gone also was the bowl of traditional homemade eggnog. My father used to make it, but when we talked about getting the ingredients, my brother said it always tasted like creme-colored hand lotion. Surprisingly, we all agreed. So we didn't make it.

We got through Christmas that year with nearly the normal number of laughs. But something was decidedly different, and as we packed up to go back to California a few days later, I felt a little sad, like a homesick child filled with a longing for the stability of a home that didn't really exist.

Maybe it was a larger grief over all the changes in my life. Though I was grown up, I still felt childlike longings for stability. I resisted change. My father's death and absence seemed only a foretaste of life's inevitable changes ahead of me.

Though I had worried about my mother's response to grief and change, maybe the problem was mine too. Maybe I didn't know how to deal with the homesick longing in my heart.

On a cold and blustery Thanksgiving morning nearly eighteen years later, I woke up with that same homesick feeling in my heart.

On this Thanksgiving I was dealing with another kind of hole in my family. It was the first holiday without Derek, our oldest, who was a freshman in college far away and not able to come home. Somehow we had endured the good-bye on the college campus and the ensuing months of his absence, but the reality of his empty place at our Thanksgiving table seemed painfully symbolic of the major change in our family.

We had always been a family of five: five faces in the Christmas card pictures, five bodies climbing into the car to visit grandparents, five names on the phone answering machine messages, five places around the table. Now we were four.

I got up early and put the twenty-pound turkey in the oven. I scrubbed potatoes and checked the ingredients for the traditional vegetable casserole. But I put off setting the table. I simply didn't want to do it. I hadn't gotten the dusty box of Thanksgiving decorations out of the garage either.

Around midmorning, Kendall, at twelve our youngest, wandered into the kitchen, rubbing the sleep out of her eyes.

"It's starting to smell good," she said, "but it sure doesn't look much like Thanksgiving around here. This place needs some decorations."

She probably sensed my sadness and feared my mood might signal the end to Thanksgivings around our house the way she knew them. So she went into action.

Kendall has always had a knack for creating something artistic and interesting out of nearly nothing, and I watched in wonder as she pulled some fruit and vegetables out of the refrigerator and made a centerpiece. She added some candles, and then stood back to survey the room.

"Not enough," she declared.

Next she began rummaging through some drawers and came across some shiny aluminum cookie cutters.

"Aha!" she said. Then she pulled out some dental floss, fetched a wire coat hanger from the hall closet, untwisted it, and tied five people-shaped cookie cutters together on it, creating an instant mobile.

"There!" she said. "Our family."

She then hung the mobile in a window, where the five shapes danced around crazily in the sunlight. "See, Derek's not here, but he's still attached," she said, pulling one cookie cutter away from the rest. As she pulled the "Derek" shape away, the others danced around crazily, totally out of whack. But after a bit, they all settled down again.

As Kendall left the room, I marveled at the lesson she'd just demonstrated. When change happens—when the absence of one family member leaves a hole in the structure—the family mobile wobbles around crazily for awhile. It's a time of transition. Things feel out of whack. Sad feelings might surface. Coping seems difficult. There's a longing for stability.

But things don't stay out of whack. Eventually everyone settles down again. Maybe not in the same place or pattern. Maybe in a new configuration. But the people are still connected.

As I gazed at the mobile dancing in the sun, I remembered back to that first Christmas after my father died, and my response to my mother's Mine Shaft. My mother wasn't obsessed with saving junk;

she was merely going through that out-of-whack period of adjustment, and The Mine Shaft was her way of coping. Kind of like my
reluctance to set the table or put up Thanksgiving decorations.

As for the change in family traditions that Christmas, I wish
I'd been more gracious and gentle in my responses. Since then, I've
learned that we should hold on to family traditions loosely, not
rigidly. We should enjoy them while they are meaningful and let go
of them as we outgrow them.

When I put these two holidays together, that Christmas without my father and the Thanksgiving without Derek, and add what
I've learned through the years about the character of God and his
plan for us, I see what we can learn from experiences like these.

I see how change is an inevitable part of the pattern of our lives.
The shape of families change, circumstances change, holiday traditions change. And our response to change can help us recognize our
longing for God, because he never changes. Our longing for stability is satisfied as we draw closer to him and believe his promise, that
though we face changes and losses and disappointments in this
world, he remains constant.

He also knits that feeling of homesickness into our hearts for
a reason. It is the homesickness I first noticed the Christmas after my
father died—a longing for a consistently secure and loving and
never-changing home that doesn't exist here on earth. It is a longing that is keenly revealed to us when we return to the home of our
childhood or look at an empty place at our family table and find that
things aren't quite the same. And we begin to realize that they never
will be.

This homesickness is a bittersweet longing that points us to
God, who promises us a home in heaven that never changes. And
God is calling us home.

Footprint Scripture

I the LORD *do not change (Mal. 3:6).*

Footprint Lessons

- Change is an inevitable part of our lives that brings temporary periods of adjustment, especially in families. Be gentle with each other during times of change.

- Hold on loosely, not tightly, to family traditions. They will change as families grow and change.

- The longing we feel during times of change is knit into our hearts by God. It is a longing for him . . . and for a home called heaven.

Reflections

1. What are some of the major losses or changes you have faced in your life? Describe the feelings of adjustment. What longings did you experience?

2. If you have lost a parent or someone close to you, how has that loss impacted your family structure and traditions?

3. How have your family traditions changed over the years?

4. God promises that he never changes. What does this mean to you? How have you sensed his never-changing presence in times of change?

5. What does it mean to "long for heaven"?

four

Sibling Comparisons

Am I in second place?

When Lynn got out of the Navy in California, we moved back to Colorado, and I soon found myself taking care of our three young children in the same hometown where I grew up. Meanwhile, my older sister was living in Hollywood, pursuing a glamorous career in television. For years, she played the role of Valene in the long-running series, *Knots Landing*. She often starred in television movies and appeared on prime-time talk shows.

Her name is Joan Van Ark, and she got lots of "hometown-girl-makes-good" coverage in our local newspaper. No wonder I often got questions about why we seemed so different.

"What was it like, growing up with a famous sister?" the checkout lady at the grocery store asked one day as she pushed my package of disposable diapers across her scanner and motioned to the *TV Guide* with my sister's picture on the cover. "Was it difficult for you?"

Though I'd gotten to know this checkout lady pretty well, I didn't know how to answer her questions. Did she wonder whether I felt like I was in second place? Or, as I stood there bouncing a cranky baby on one hip while trying to keep the other two children from grabbing candy off the nearby racks, did she wonder if I envied my sister's place in life . . . or questioned my own? Was she hoping I'd confess some secret resentment?

I longed for some profound answers, but I had none. So as I fumbled for my checkbook and commanded my four- and five-year-old children to "freeze" (my code word for "stand still!"), I merely smiled.

"The only time I really resented my sister and our different places in life was the day my grandfather exploded a greasy chicken all over our kitchen," I told her. "And I decided it was all Joan's fault, even though she wasn't there."

"Sounds juicy," the checkout lady said with a grin as she put my bags into the cart and looked at the line of people behind me. "You'll have to tell me about it sometime."

"Mommy," four-year-old Lindsay tugged my arm as we wheeled the cart across the parking lot, "how did a chicken explode?"

After I loaded the groceries into the car and strapped the children into their seats, I gave them a condensed version of the chicken fiasco.

To set the scene and tell the whole story, I actually have to start back before the chicken explosion. I grew up second in the birth order of our family of four children, underneath Joan. From the beginning, Joan appeared to fit the mold of the classic firstborn over-achiever. She always knew she wanted to be an actress when she grew up.

She started fulfilling that dream by making up and directing plays when we were about four and six. Somehow she always cast herself as the beautiful princess and assigned me the supporting role, like the ugly stepsister. My younger brothers usually got cast as props, like dogs or tables. I didn't think much about the inequity of our roles then; after all, one of the undisputed privileges of being the oldest is that you get to be the boss.

Joan and I got along pretty well as teenagers. When she turned sixteen, she drove me places, especially if I bribed her by paying for gas. We shared clothes and learned to count on each other. I missed her when she graduated and went off to New York City to pursue her career—until the day of the chicken fiasco.

Like I said, Joan wasn't there. Neither were my mother and father. Joan had some important audition in New York City and my parents had gone back east to be with her. They thought they'd covered the bases at home, getting my grandfather to come stay with me and my two younger brothers. I was glad for his help because I was in charge of the high school homecoming decorations that weekend.

On Saturday, the day of the big dance, I needed to gather autumn leaves and make fake trees in the school auditorium all day. Gumpy (as we used to call my grandfather) assured me he had everything under control. For dinner, he planned to make his specialty— fricasseed chicken in the pressure cooker—for my two younger brothers. I detested pressure cookers because of the hissing sound they made, but I wouldn't be there anyway.

I rushed home about five o'clock that afternoon with just enough time to change and get ready for the big dance. My grandfather, who was a bit hard of hearing, was in another part of the house. He didn't know the pressure cooker was hissing more loudly than usual, kind of like it was ready to blow up.

"Gumpy!" I called out from the hallway, but I barely got his name out when—sure enough!—the pressure cooker exploded all over the kitchen, spewing greasy chicken on the ceiling, across the windows, and up into the cupboard filled with dishes and glasses. I took one look at the mess and wanted to walk out of that house forever.

"Oh mercy," my grandfather sputtered as he came in and surveyed the mess. "That shouldn't have happened."

As I saw the pathetic, helpless look on my grandfather's face, one thing became clear. Gumpy didn't do greasy kitchens. Neither did my two younger brothers, who were conveniently missing at that moment. Only one person seemed capable of cleaning up that mess before it solidified, and that person suddenly had a heart filled with resentment.

Thank heavens my resentment gave me energy.

For the next two hours, I scraped up chicken chunks and washed every blasted greasy glass and plate in the cupboard, which gave me plenty of time to wallow in my resentment. I resented my sister . . . and the fact that she was in New York and I wasn't . . . and my parents

... and their priorities ... and their lack of understanding about the importance of my responsibility to make fake trees ... and the decision to leave my grandfather in charge ... and pressure cookers ... and chicken ... and the fact we had too many glasses in our cupboard ... and God for allowing me to be the second-born and to be still living at home. I pretty well covered all the bases, and actually felt good about conjuring up so much legitimate self-pity.

Later that night at the homecoming dance, with the lingering fragrance of greasy chicken still on my hands, I told anyone who would listen about the chicken explosion at our house. I admit I began to embellish the story a bit, but everyone loved it, including me. By the end of the evening, I'd pretty much run out of resentment.

Or had I? I wondered as the sounds of my three children, strapped into their car seats all around me, brought me back to the present. Derek and Lindsay were arguing over a box of animal crackers, and Kendall, the baby, had a dirty diaper. In the trunk were eight sacks of groceries that needed to be put away in a kitchen already littered with sticky juice cups and almost-empty boxes of cereal.

The chicken story didn't really answer the questions about the differences between me and my sister. It may have been an example of dealing with a *moment* of resentment, but how did my place in *life* compare to hers?

The questions still lingered.

Today, at age fifty, I have some better answers. They didn't come to me in a single dramatic moment. They evolved slowly as I continued to wonder about my place in life, especially in comparison to my sister.

One learning experience started with a phone call on a snowy, cold January day.

"I'll get it," came the chorus from all over the house.

"Mom, it's Joan!"

My sister sounded excited when I picked up the extension. "Carol, they want us to be on the *Today Show* together next week."

"No way . . . I couldn't . . . who's *they*"? I sputtered.

"It will be great," Joan chattered on, and then explained. *They* were the *Today Show* producers who were interested that I was mostly a mom and sometimes a writer who worked at home and lived in the same town where Joan and I grew up.

"They want to know why we're so different," Joan said.

There was that question again.

"Geez, Joan, I don't think so . . . I don't like flying alone. I don't have a clue what to wear. And I don't know what I'd say in the interview."

"You'll be great. We'll get all the details worked out. I'll meet you at the airport. We'll have fun."

Before I knew it, the details were worked out and I was on my way to New York. Joan met me at the airport and a limousine delivered us to a downtown hotel. About 5 A.M. the next morning, a hair and makeup person showed up at our hotel room door with curling irons and hair dryers dangling from his belt. He carried a large fishing tackle box loaded with makeup. For the next hour, he poofed our hair and painted our faces with brushes, like some paint-by-number project. When he finished, I looked in the mirror and hardly recognized myself. I thought that if I sneezed, my whole face might come off.

The phone rang, announcing that another limousine had arrived, and we were off for a three-block ride to Rockefeller Plaza. Into an elevator, up several floors to another makeup room where some other people checked our makeup and then ushered us into the *Today Show* studio where I ran smack dab into the weatherman Willard Scott.

"How's the weather?" I asked with a grin, smugly proud of myself for being so cleverly appropriate. Maybe this TV stuff was going to be fun. Little did I know, that was about the last full sentence I would utter in that studio.

We were directed to some chairs in a corner of the studio. Bright lights; sound check; Bryant Gumbel appeared. Joan knew him. They chatted briefly. I said hello. Countdown . . . *Five . . . four . . . three . . . two . . . one.* We were on. Everybody talked at once. Big smiles. A few laughs.

In the blink of an eye, it was over. Then it was back down in the elevator; back to the hotel; pack up and back to the airport; hugs; back to Colorado; and home to the house in the same town where I grew up.

"Welcome home, Mom!"

"The show was great, Mom! Can you help me with my Spanish vocabulary tonight?"

"Guess what, Mom. I slept through it. Sorry."

That night as I scrubbed the makeup off my face, I knew I'd just had an incredible adventure. But I felt thankful to be home.

Am I in second place . . . or the right place? The answer, I now realize, has less to do with circumstances and more to do with an attitude of trust in God who created me. It's not about yearning for the ways things might be; it's about being content with the way things are.

As for comparisons, sure my sister and I are very different. With three children of my own, I appreciate with greater awareness how God creates each of us uniquely different and then uses those differences for his unique purposes. The differences between Joan and me bring us closer together. We don't compete; we complement each other. We fill in each other's spaces. Sometimes she stretches me in directions I need to go; other times I do the same for her. But different means just plain *different*, not better.

As for being in second place, in God's great scheme there is no such thing as first or second place. Only the right place. God, who knows the end from the beginning and who knit each of us together in our mothers' wombs, has been working out his divine purposes for each of us since before we were born.

That means he goes before us each step of the way. He orchestrates just the right circumstances for our growth toward him and his purposes for us. He places us in the right places in our families or in the world to help us grow into the person he created each of us to be.

There's great comfort and security in believing God's promises about being in the right place in life. I can find contentment in the place where I am instead of questioning it, knowing God has something for me in this place. It is the right place right now.

I can look to the future with excitement, knowing he is growing me toward another place that he is saving for me.

I don't have to compare my place to anyone else's place because no one else jeopardizes the security of my place.

Yet, if a little resentment creeps in now and then as we compare our place to another's place in life, maybe God allows that too, because recognizing our resentment can help us recognize our need to trust him. As I look back on the famous chicken fiasco, I see that I learned something about dealing with resentment about my place in life. It helps to talk about resentment, maybe even wallow in it for a short time. But then we need to let go of it, knowing that no one, or nothing else, forces us into second place or the wrong place. God is saving just the right place for us. And he grows us toward that place through challenges along the way.

Finally, those are the right answers to the questions about my place in life.

Footprint Scripture

Before I formed you in the womb I knew you,
before you were born I set you apart (Jer.1:5).

Footprint Lessons

- God, who knows the end from the beginning, has been working out his purposes for our lives since before we were born. He creates us uniquely to fulfill his unique purposes for our lives.

- We do not have to worry about our place in life. God saves just the right place for us, and where we are today is preparing us for that place.

- Our circumstances are helping us grow into the person God created us to be.

- Comparisons about first and second place don't exist in God's scheme. Each person's place is secure—in life and in eternity. Besides, someone else's goodness does not diminish our goodness in God's eyes. And different means *different*, not better.

- If we feel some resentment about our place in life, we should look at that resentment, talk to God about it, and then let go of it.

Reflections

1. How are you and your siblings different? How are your own children different from each other?

2. Have you ever resented your differences? Explain.

3. How have your differences helped you become the person you are today? How has God used your differences for his purposes?

4. When have you resented or questioned your place in life?

5. How do you handle resentment?

6. How is God growing you in the place where you are right now?

part two

Adjusting to Transitions

He will not let your foot slip . . .
Psalm 121:3

Life is filled with transitions; bridges between what was and what will be. Sometimes those bridges seem wobbly, insecure, or risky, because we have to leave where we've been in order to reach the place where we are going. We have to let go of the past before we can fully embrace the future.

We don't stay on these bridges of transition; they are temporary, in-between places of growing and becoming. However, we don't notice our growth until we reach the other side and look back. Only then do we realize that God has put those bridges in our paths, and has walked with us across the span of uncertain territory to security on the other side.

five

Married Love

*How do we get
to "happily ever after"?*

As our June wedding date neared, Lynn and I excitedly counted the days and checked the necessary items off our prenuptial "to do" list.

Find a photographer.

Send out invitations.

Order the cake.

Meet with minister for premarital counseling.

This last item merely seemed like one more obligation squeezed in between so many others. We didn't feel the need for much help or advice. Friends told us we were perfectly matched. And I loved almost everything about Lynn, especially the way his calm and logical approach to life balanced my more emotional responses.

Naturally, we assumed that if we hit any snags in our future, the bliss of being married would take care of everything. After all, love conquers all, and marriage means living "happily ever after," right? How could we expect otherwise when it starts with a storybook ceremony described with romantic words like *bride and groom* . . . *wedding bells*. . . and *honeymoon*?

Our minister must have recognized our idealism as we sat in his office that bright spring day for our counseling session. Maybe he attributed it to our age: Lynn was twenty-three, and I was twenty-one, fresh out of college.

"You know, marriage is pretty wonderful," he smiled as he leaned across his desk, "but it's also lots of hard work, especially in the beginning. My wife and I have been married for fifteen years, and we wouldn't trade places with newlyweds for anything! You're going to face some surprising adjustments as you begin to realize that neither one of you is perfect."

I nodded and smiled on the outside, but on the inside I made a staunch vow: We would be different.

The minister then explained that he always read the "love chapter"—1 Corinthians 13—in wedding ceremonies. "If you hold that definition of love before you," he assured us, "it will help you build your marriage."

Actually, I was more concerned with the "how to's" of the wedding ceremony than the "how to's" of building a marriage. My priorities focused on how to walk down the aisle in step with my father, pass the ring without dropping it, and get up from a kneeling position without tripping on my dress. How to build a marriage would take care of itself.

How naive of me.

This same wise minister had barely pronounced us husband and wife before we faced some testing of our vows in the marriage-building process. We went to a beachside hotel for our honeymoon, where Lynn got so badly sunburned on our first day that he couldn't even wear shoes. He felt miserable, so I had an opportunity to work on the "in sickness and in health" vow.

We worked on the "for richer or for poorer" vow when we arrived at the New York City airport a few days later and hailed a taxi to get to my grandparents' empty apartment, where we would stay overnight. We sat in the back seat of the cab and watched in amazement—and then panic—as the numbers on the meter kept clicking upwards, tallying a fare that soon got way beyond the amount of cash in our pockets. The sign on the meter clearly stated "Cash Only."

How could we run out of money before the end of our honeymoon? I wondered. Thanks heavens for a trusting doorman at the apartment building, who lent us some cash.

We got the opportunity to work on "for better or for worse" many times during our first year as we meshed our two lifestyles together and began to recognize our differences. Take our differing standards of cleanliness, for instance. To me, clean meant the absence of clutter in plain sight, or clean on the outside. To Lynn, clean meant orderly on the inside, such as tidy closets and drawers. With great gusto, he'd clean out our bedroom closet by pulling everything out and putting only two-thirds back in. This left the closet looking orderly but the room in total disaster, with separate piles everywhere: one for the cleaners, one for giving away, one to reconsider later.

Piles didn't bother Lynn, even if they stayed in plain sight for days. To him, they indicated a work in progress.

Piles irritated me.

I also began to see silly little things I had never noticed before we got married. Like how differently we drove. Lynn approached stale green lights slowly, waiting for them to change to yellow. I liked to speed up and zoom through them, daring them to change. As we slowed down at intersection after intersection I thought we should zoom through, I began to recognize something about myself. I was extremely impatient. And Lynn was not.

There were other small differences. I assumed when he went to the grocery store, he would never bring home pink toilet paper. And when we had a disagreement, I preferred immediate, face-to-face discussions. He liked to step back and see if the whole thing would blow over.

It's funny how the accumulation of little things can grow monstrously big and out of proportion sometimes. By the time Lynn and I opened the freezer and pulled out the box containing the top of our wedding cake to celebrate our first anniversary, we'd had some wonderful times—and faced some times of testing.

Even though we'd been warned, those testing times surprised me.

Last Sunday in church, the pastor asked an elderly couple to stand.

"This fine couple is celebrating their sixty-seventh wedding anniversary today, so we want to acknowledge that great milestone and thank them for being an inspiration to all of us."

Turning to the couple, he asked, "Before you sit down, do you have any advice about the secrets of success in marriage?"

The gentleman tenderly put his arm around his wife and said in a strong voice, "The greatest investment a married couple can make is their investment in God and each other."

An envious "ahhh" of appreciation quietly rippled across the congregation as people responded to the time-tested devotion of this couple.

I glanced over at Lynn, who was sitting beside me, because this man's advice reminded me of what our minister had told us in that memorable premarital counseling session twenty-eight years earlier. Though the words were different, the message was the same. And it was a message I understood a lot better now: Times of testing of the marriage vows will come, but marriage gets better when you keep investing in God and each other.

Translated into a piece of advice, here it is: Hang in there. Don't give up, especially as you learn to work through your differences in the early years of marriage. Great goodness and strength can grow out of that vow-testing as the innocence of young love is replaced by something much richer and deeper.

Coincidentally, I've been thinking lots lately about the secrets of success and longevity in building a long-lasting marriage. I supposed this is not only because we are approaching our twenty-ninth wedding anniversary, but because our own children are reaching marriageable age in a world where the divorce rate runs nearly neck-and-neck with the success rate of marriage.

So I've been reflecting back on our own experiences, just in case our children ask us about what matters most in marriage.

Though I know such requests happen mostly in a mother's dreams, I'm ready. And this is what I would tell them.

First, pick the right person as your mate. This is obvious, but obviously not simple. It is a matter of prayer and discernment, of a decision pondered and tested through time, and of premarital counseling, hopefully taken more seriously than we had. Our church offers a "Before You Buy the Ring" seminar for couples considering marriage. That's a good time to look at the issues, because once a couple is engaged, they are already committed and distracted by the responsibilities of planning a wedding ceremony.

Second, accept your mate as the right person for you. After marriage, accept that person for being the *right* person, not a *perfect* person. As a friend told me, "I spent a long time expecting my husband to be Mr. Perfect. As soon as I realized there is no Mr. Perfect, life got a whole lot easier and I started loving him for being Mr. Right." I've also learned that it's not the big things that destroy a marriage as much as the accumulation of little things as two people struggle to accept each other's imperfections and quirky habits. When I quit expecting Lynn to be just like me, I started accepting and appreciating him for who he is.

Third, invest in your mate. The secret of loving another person is to care more about that person's happiness than your own. This means knowing what pleases the other person, and choosing that. It means doing whatever brings out the best in the other person. It means cherishing the other person and showing a continual commitment to work at building the marriage so the other person knows he or she is worth the effort.

Fourth, keep remembering why you married your mate. Get out the wedding pictures often—at least every anniversary. Remind yourself of those traits that drew you together. At every wedding you attend, listen to the vows and vicariously remarry each other.

Finally, put God in your marriage. Our minister told us to hold on to 1 Corinthians 13 so that we would recognize our dependence upon God as we built our marriage. I didn't have a clue what he meant at the time, but I've learned through the years. Love may start with romantic feelings and blissful dreams but marriages are built through time as two people learn that commitment means living out their vows and aiming for a 1 Corinthians 13 kind of love.

Love never gives up.
Love cares more for others than for self.

Love doesn't want what it doesn't have. . . .
Isn't always "me first" . . .
Puts up with anything,
Trusts God always,
Always looks for the best,
Never looks back,
But keeps going to the end.

1 Corinthians 13 THE MESSAGE

Most of us are not capable of consistently living out that kind of love on our own. At least, that's what marriage has revealed to me about myself. I now see that 1 Corinthians 13 is not a "how to" chapter as much as a "point to" chapter. It points me to God, the only source of perfect love. I recognize my dependence upon him as I aim to become a vessel of that kind of perfect love. And as I love God more, I love my husband more.

I once saw a drawing illustrating a marriage that points to God. It was a triangle with God at the top point and the husband and wife at the bottom two corners, inching their way up the sides of the triangle. The caption read, "The closer we grow to God, the closer we grow to each other."

If our children ask for advice about marriage, I'll share these reflections. But I'm also realistic about the impact of such advice. Like Lynn and me, they may hear the words, but they'll probably have to learn many of these lessons for themselves.

Still, the exercise of gathering the advice has been good for me. It reminds me of why I married Lynn in the first place . . . because I love almost everything about him. It also reminds me that marriage does get better, and that it's well worth the investment. And it helps me respond with fonder patience when we slow down at stale green lights.

Which we still do.

Footprint Scripture

Love comes from God . . . (1 John 4:7).

Footprint Lessons

- Marriage is a relationship with great potential for growth.

- Marriage gets better through the years as we learn to invest in God and in each other.

- Love starts with romantic feelings and blissful dreams, but marriages are built upon a choice of commitment as two people learn to live out their wedding vows and the description of love in 1 Corinthians 13.

- Accept your mate; don't expect to change him.

- A husband and wife grow closer to each other as they grow closer to God. The more you love God, the more you will love your mate.

Reflections

1. What qualities drew you to your spouse in the first place? How do you still affirm those qualities?

2. How was your first year of marriage? What were some of your unrealistic expectations?

3. How has your marriage changed since the day you got married? How have you weathered some of your transitions? What have you learned?

4. Read 1 Corinthians 13. What part of that definition of love is most difficult for you? What part comes most naturally?

5. If you are not married, how do you live out this definition of love in the primary relationships in your life?

6. How might you treat your spouse (or others) differently, based on the verses in 1 Corinthians 13?

7. What one piece of advice would you pass on to a friend getting ready to be married?

six

Home Alone
My world is closing in

One hot summer morning, my golden retriever, Rhody, nuzzled me awake with her cold, wet nose. Already the air felt heavy and muggy, and at seven months pregnant, I felt huge. The house seemed quiet, and I realized Lynn had left for work without waking me. I should have been grateful for his consideration, but his gesture only increased my incredible sense of loneliness.

Lynn and I had just moved to San Diego. He was in the Navy, and since I was due to deliver our first child in a couple of months, we had decided I would not look for a job. Instead, I would seek free-lance writing projects I could do at home. This decision marked a huge transition in my life, because I had never been at home full-time. Yet here I was, just me and the dog, every day, all day long.

I thought I would like this new opportunity. I imagined myself reading all the books I'd never had time to tackle or immersed in home-decorating projects like refinishing furniture and matting pictures to brighten up our sparse little rental unit. I even fancied myself becoming a great cook and actually using some of the recipes I'd been clipping out of magazines and newspapers for years.

Yet I found myself feeling strangely listless and burdened by a growing feeling of loneliness. I blamed it on the mood swings of my pregnancy and the newness of this stage of life. For the first time, I had no structure to define my day. Nor did I have any people around me. Since grade school, I'd always been part of some larger context of potential friends, such as a class of students or a staff at work. I missed that sense of belonging.

"What shall we do today, Rhody?" I asked the dog as she followed me through the empty house to the kitchen.

How pathetic, I thought as I poured myself a glass of juice. *I'm turning into one of those people who has nothing better to do than talk to her dog all day long.*

I looked around the kitchen and suddenly got an idea: I would surprise Lynn with a gourmet lunch, something special we could eat outside. The more I thought about it, the more I liked the idea, so I found some music on the radio, turned up the volume, and then opened the drawer with the stash of recipes. I needed a lunch-something, and one for which I had the ingredients, since Lynn had our only car.

It was almost 10:30 by the time I had decided upon a recipe for baked tuna croquettes and pulled out all the ingredients. I didn't especially like tuna fish, but Lynn did, so I started washing and chopping onions and celery, and mixing up the tuna fish, and setting the picnic table on our little backyard porch. Lynn usually came home a bit after noon and had about forty-five minutes for lunch. He didn't come home *every* day, but he'd be glad he'd made the trip today.

By noon, the tuna croquettes were piping hot and smelled good. I covered them with some foil, poured homemade tea over the ice cubes in some tall glasses, and set everything on the table. I then busied myself cleaning up while I waited for Lynn. And waited. At 12:20, I started feeling a bit disappointed. Lynn would have to rush through lunch in order to be back in his office by 1 P.M.

By 12:30, I started to get irritated. Sometimes he ran late, but this seemed inconsiderate. The tuna croquettes were growing colder, and the ice cubes had melted. So I went to the phone and dialed his number. After three long rings, he answered.

"Hi," he said cheerfully. "I was down the hall getting a sandwich out of the machine. I'm working through lunch because we have an important meeting at one o'clock. I was about to call and see how your day is going."

"I thought you were coming home for lunch," I stammered into the phone.

"Oh, I'm sorry," he answered. "I told you I wasn't coming home when I said good-bye this morning. I thought you were awake, but I guess you didn't hear me."

"I guess not. . . ."

"I'll see you about six o'clock tonight."

I hung up the phone and stared at the receiver. I felt like crying, but the tears didn't come. I couldn't blame Lynn. This wasn't his fault. But as I marched into the kitchen, I wasn't quite sure what to do with my feelings. Rhody faithfully followed me, sat down, and wagged her tail as I stood looking at the tuna croquettes. On a sudden impulse, I picked up the pan and dumped the croquettes into the dog's dish. In a few seconds, she had gobbled them up and was back at my side, looking up at me approvingly.

"Did you enjoy those?" I asked.

Here I go again. Talking to the dog. How pathetic.

Then I sat down on the floor and cried.

A few months ago, on a clear September morning, I walked through an empty house, followed only by our two-year-old golden retriever, Boaz. Kendall, our youngest, had just left for college, and the reality of her being gone was starting to sink in. We now lived in an Empty Nest, that famous quiet place in the life of a family where the house grows still because the children have all left home. It was a mixed-up place of transition, but I had been in similar places before—not exactly the same circumstances maybe, but with the burden of similar feelings.

Like the time after our move to San Diego when I felt so lonely in that new community before our first child was born. Or the day I made that gourmet lunch for Lynn and then fed it to the dog when

Lynn didn't show up. It was that day I learned something about how God meets us in those moments when we don't know what to do with the burden of our mixed-up feelings.

I remembered sitting down on the floor and crying that day. But I also remembered that, in my rock-bottom moment of frustration, I reached some realizations.

I realized that I shouldn't be so dependent upon Lynn to meet all my needs. No one person can completely meet another's emotional needs. To expect that of a husband or friend or parents puts an unfair burden on that person. And that unrealistic expectation wasn't good for me either.

In my loneliness, I also recognized I couldn't stay inside my house and wait for someone to appear out of nowhere and knock on the door or call me on the phone. The walls of the world close in on a person who chooses that kind of isolation.

I knew I needed to take some initiative in order to find a sense of belonging in this new community. I needed to seek some new friends by looking for existing structures of potential friends. I needed to muster up the courage to step outside the walls of my own home.

That courage came to me as I sat on the kitchen floor that day. Not merely out of the thin air, but out of a time of talking to God. For in that rock-bottom moment, I prayed. It wasn't an on-my-knees prayer, said in formal prayer language to "my Father who art in heaven;" instead, it was an open-hearted confession of my loneliness and mixed-up feelings.

After that time of prayer, I felt less burdened. I got up, washed my face, and then walked several blocks down to the recreation center, where I signed up for an exercise class for pregnant women.

In addition to realizing a few things about myself in that experience, I also learned something about God: He knows everything. He knows about the burden of our feelings in times of difficult transitions, but he still desires that we turn to him and talk to him about those mixed-up feelings. Such open-hearted prayer conversations don't change him, and they may not change our circumstances, but in those moments of openness, God changes *us*. He lifts our burdens and strengthens us as he reveals his nearness.

He also acknowledges our feelings. "I know you're lonely [or confused, or tired, or frustrated]," he says to us. "I know you're unsure about what to do and where to turn. Turn to me. Trust me. I understand. I'll take your hand. I'll walk with you. I'll carry the burden of your feelings for today. Together, we'll find someone else who needs a friend. "

Through the years, the settings and circumstances of my transitional times have changed: adjusting to life in a new community; learning to cope with three young children in a perpetually noisy and messy house; feeling all alone in a quiet, empty house. But in the middle of each transition—when the confusion and loneliness grow bigger and the walls start closing in—I open-heartedly confess my feelings to God and begin to sense his nearness: "I know. I understand. I'll walk with you. I'll carry your burdens for today." In my time of prayer, he transforms me. He lightens the burden of my mixed-up feelings and gives me courage and strength.

I don't understand how or why it works. But I don't have to understand. I only have to believe God, and then *act* like I believe him. That's why, on that recent day when I walked through an empty house filled with memories of children now gone and felt the growing burden of loneliness and mixed-up feelings, I knew where to turn.

A dog is a great companion, but God alone can lift the burden of my feelings.

Footprint Scripture

Come to me, all you who are weary and burdened,
and I will give you rest. . . . For my yoke is easy and
my burden is light (Matt. 11:28, 30).

Footprint Lessons

- When we give our burdens to God, he carries them for us.

- Our open-hearted prayers do not change God, and they may not change our circumstances; but in our prayer time, we are changed. When we confess our feelings of brokeness to God, he changes us.

- When loneliness descends and the walls of our world begin to close in on us, God gives us the courage to step outside the walls of our isolation.

- No one person can meet all our emotional needs. To expect that puts an unfair burden on that person.

Reflections

1. When have you experienced a situation in which you built up some expectations about the way your plans would work out, but they did not work that way? What did you learn from that experience?

2. Is there one person in your life upon whom you could depend to meet most of your needs? In what ways might that put an unfair burden on that person?

3. Can you describe a time of loneliness in your life? What did you do about your loneliness?

4. How has God used your loneliness to draw you to him? Looking back, what kind of spiritual growth came out of your loneliness?

5. What does it mean to you to "cast your burdens on the Lord"?

Becoming a Mom

I thought kisses took care of everything

The clock said 3 A.M.

It was our first night home from the hospital with our newborn baby, Derek, and there I sat, nervously rocking him. But he wouldn't stop whimpering. He obviously needed something I didn't know how to give him, and I felt confused.

I thought becoming a mother would be easy. I thought that, instantly and instinctively, I would know how to take care of my child. I thought hugs and kisses would stop his crying.

Obviously, I was wrong.

So now Lynn and I were taking a middle-of-the-night crash course in How to Parent.

"Lynn, what do we do for hiccups?" I asked anxiously.

"Hiccups . . . let's see," Lynn said as he sat on the bed, flipping through the pages of a book on child care. "Hiccups are fairly common during infancy," he read. "Pat the baby's back gently to bubble him."

"Bubble him? What does that mean?" I asked. "Oh no, now he's spitting up."

"Spitting up . . ." Lynn repeated, as he started flipping through the pages again.

Even as I gently patted Derek's back, he continued to whimper.

Mentally, I started to review the full round of possible solutions again.

Was he hungry? In the hospital, I learned that breastfed babies might need to eat as often as every two hours at first. But I didn't know if that meant two hours from the beginning or ending of the last feeding. If it meant from the beginning, maybe this whimpering child was hungry again.

Meanwhile, Lynn started reading about the difference between demand feeding (determined by the baby) and scheduled feeding (determined by the parents). From the descriptions, it sounded like this single decision could influence who would rule our home for the next eighteen years—the child or the parents.

"Oh no," I moaned, as I headed to the changing table for a dry diaper. That's when Derek's whimpers turned into real cries.

"Look under *crying*, Lynn," I begged.

"Soon you'll distinguish between the 'I'm hungry' cry and the 'I'm tired' cry," Lynn read.

"Distinguish!" I repeated. "This is the first time I've heard him really cry."

"Practically every baby has a regular crying period at about the same time each day," Lynn continued.

"Swell," I answered. "He's picked three o'clock in the morning."

"The severity and duration of the crying is usually directly proportional to the tension, confusion, and turmoil in the home."

"We've got all three," I acknowledged wearily.

"Maybe it's too bright in here," Lynn decided, and with that, he began rearranging the lighting system in the room, moving lamps, bringing in new light bulbs and extension chords. Finally, the baby fell asleep. Probably out of sheer exhaustion. We felt exhausted too, so I gently placed Derek back in his bassinet and we crawled into bed and turned out the light. Lynn fell asleep immediately, but I couldn't. Though my body ached with fatigue, my mind seemed set on "baby alert," a new kind of consciousness.

Suddenly, the room seemed too quiet; I couldn't hear Derek breathing. I listened intently for a few seconds, then jumped out of bed, flipped the light back on, crept over to the bassinet, and put my hand on his back. I must have startled him, because he began whimpering again.

Immediately, I picked him up.

Maybe he's hungry. With that I started back through the round of options once again. Eating. Burping. Changing.

Lynn slept through this round, so as I sat there rocking the fretful baby, I looked around at how we had so carefully prepared for him before he was born: the garage-sale changing table, freshly painted and stocked with all the necessary supplies; the bassinet with a ruffley new cover; the bright and whimsical mobile, guaranteed to stimulate and develop his curiosity.

Physically, I had prepared for our baby's coming, but how could I have prepared emotionally to face the awesome responsibility of caring for an infant who would be totally dependent upon me? That assignment of carrying an egg around for two weeks in a Life Skills class in high school didn't prepare me. Eggs don't cry.

The truth is, I was a better mom before I had a baby. In my imagination, at least I knew how to make my baby stop crying.

I don't know how long Derek and I sat there in that big rocking chair, but we both must have fallen asleep, because Lynn's alarm jolted me awake at 6 A.M. Lynn got out of bed, gently placed the baby back in the bassinet, and helped me to bed.

I fell back to sleep as the sun began to rise.

Later, when I went downstairs for a cup of coffee, I found that Lynn had left one of our child care books open on the kitchen table before he went to work. He had marked this passage: "When an infant has been awake an unusually long while or stimulated by being played with by his parents, he may become irritable. Instead of being easier for him to fall sleep, it may be harder. If the parent then tries to comfort him with more talk and bouncing around, it only acts as more stimulation and may make matters worse . . ."

Obviously, I had made matters worse. How would I ever learn to be a good mother? Right then, the task seemed impossible.

I am now nearing the end of my years of active parenting. Our almost-adult children merely pop in and out of our Empty Nest these days. No wonder I get nostalgic and often remember back to the beginning of my mothering days, especially that memorable first night home from the hospital with our first child. I smile now as I recall that frantic night. I am convinced God gave me that baptism-by-fire initiation into motherhood as a preview of several truths about parenting that have grown more clear through the years.

One major truth that has become very clear is that parenting is filled with unknowns. The days simply don't unfold the way we anticipate, and we don't always have the answers or know how to do what God calls us to do. We often feel like we don't know how to be good mothers.

Before our first child was born, I pictured myself being a confident, capable mother, perfectly meeting my child's needs by cuddling and comforting him. But it didn't always work that way. I couldn't always stop his crying as an infant.

Along the way, there have been many other questions with no easy answers. Questions like:

When is a child sick enough to stay home from school ... or sick enough to call the doctor?

When is saying no more important than saying yes?

How long is long enough to keep those artistic masterpieces that keep coming home from preschool?

When is it more important to let a child wear her chosen, ridiculously mismatched outfit than to suggest an alternative? What is more important, her need to gain confidence in making choices, or my need to have her look good?

Who, in yet another round of sibling rivalry, is right and who is wrong?

When is flexibility more important than consistency, or the exception more important than the rule?

When is quitting more important than sticking it out, because quitting ends an unhealthy or negative experience for the child?

When is "old enough" for your daughter to get her ears pierced?

When is "old enough" for a child to go shopping with friends ... or out on a date?

Where do I find enough patience to respond correctly when the milk spills (again) and oozes into the tablecloth that costs so much to be cleaned? Or enough patience to scratch an itch in the middle of a child's back when it keeps moving "down a little, over a little, up a little ..."?

Through the years, I've learned that being a mother means not only living with lots of unknowns, but also trusting what I *do* know in the midst of those unknowns.

This is what I do know:

I know God called me to be a mother. He gave me these three children as part of his divine plan for them and for me, and I can trust him.

I also know that when he calls us to a place or a task, he also equips and enables us for those tasks—not always instantly or instinctively, but as part of a process of growth and change. And where we make mistakes, as surely we will, we can trust him to transform even our mistakes into something good, as impossible as that may seem. For nothing is impossible with God. That's one of his promises.

It's a promise he made to two women in the Bible who, like me, stood on the threshold of motherhood, doubting their abilities to even become mothers. It seemed an impossibility to both of them. Yet God reminded them that when he called them to be mothers, he would take care of the impossibilities. He gave them that promise in which to trust—a known in the midst of unknowns.

The first woman was Sarah, the wife of Abraham, who was nearly ninety years old when God told her she would be the mother of a son. No wonder she had a hard time believing her call to motherhood and doubted she was equipped to handle this challenge. She even laughed at God. God's promise to her came in the form of a question: "Is anything too hard for the LORD?" (Gen. 18:14).

The second promise was to Mary, when the angel told her she would be the mother of Jesus. Of course Mary, a young virgin, found this nearly impossible to believe. She too felt ill-equipped! But as she adjusted to this idea, the angel gave her a promise from the Lord: "For nothing is impossible with God" (Luke 1:37).

Surely it is no coincidence that these two women, on the threshold of God's great call to motherhood, were given nearly the same promise. As mothers, God wants us to trust and believe that nothing is impossible for him. He can handle our fears and mistakes and feelings of inadequacy. When he calls us to partner with him in the divine calling of motherhood, he will equip us for that calling.

Through my years of being a mother, I've seen God's faithfulness to this promise. I've come a long way from my clumsy efforts and fears on that first night home from the hospital with Derek. I didn't ruin him that night. Of course, he doesn't even remember it. But I do, because in the midst of those inadequacies, I began to realize I couldn't face the task of mothering without God. From that very first night, I knew I needed to partner with him, trusting his promise that what I couldn't do, he could do through me.

Because nothing is impossible with him.

Footprint Scripture

*God can do anything, you know—far more than
you could ever imagine or guess or request in your
wildest dreams! He does it not by pushing us around
but by working within us, his Spirit deeply and gently within us. (Eph. 3 THE MESSAGE)*

Footprint Lessons

- When God calls us to a task such as the role of mothering, he equips and enables us for that task. When he
  gives us a responsibility, he also gives us the ability to
  carry it out.

- God partners with us each step of the way in the process
  of parenting.

- As mothers, we don't have all the answers. But God
  does. And he can transform even our mistakes into
  something good.

- God doesn't call us to be "success-full" as mothers, but
  "faith-full." He doesn't call us to be perfect, but to be
  perfectly willing to be part of the process.

- What we can't do, God can do through us . . . for nothing is impossible with God!

Reflections

1. Did you feel instantly confident in your role as a mother, or is your confidence growing slowly, as part of an ongoing process? Explain.

2. What surprised you about becoming a mother?

3. What are some of your "unknowns"? What are the questions for which you have no easy answers?

4. What is God teaching you through the role of being a mother?

5. Read God's promise to Sarah (Genesis 18:14) and to Mary (Luke 1:37). What do his promises mean to you?

6. What advice would you give a new mother who feels unsure of herself?

eight

Changing Seasons
My baby's going off to kindergarten

One memorable, crisp September morning, five-year-old Kendall, the baby of our family, marched off to kindergarten, forever closing a precious chapter of my life.

She woke up early that morning, pulled on her party dress, Velcroed on her new white tennis shoes, slipped on her backpack filled with all of her first-day-of-school necessities, and then appeared in the kitchen, where I sat drinking a cup of coffee.

"I'm ready," she announced, pulling up a stool and sitting down next to me like some suddenly-grown-up person. "What are the numbers on the clock supposed to say when it's time for the school bus, Mom?" she asked.

"Eight-oh-six," I told her.

We'd been rehearsing this scenario for days.

Obviously, she was ready, but as I looked at my precious girl-baby perched on the kitchen stool next to me, I felt a grinding in my heart—a shifting of gears—because today, when she got on that bus and headed off into a world that didn't include me, I would enter a life-altering change of seasons.

For Kendall, going off to kindergarten meant the fulfillment of a dream, born out of the envy of watching her older brother and sister go off to school each morning while she had to settle for "baby preschool," as her brother and sister teasingly called it.

For me, her going represented a bittersweet milestone. For years, I eagerly anticipated the freedom of this moment. Especially on those days when I grew weary of wiping peanut butter off high-chairs and driving preschool carpools and answering endless questions, like "How do freckles get on you?"

But now I felt a twinge of sadness as I watched her examine the carefully chosen treasures stored in her backpack. Some crayons and paper ("I'll make you a picture," she promised); a miniature purse with a quarter ("In case I need to call you"); a picture of her brother and sister ("If someone doesn't know who they are"); and a comb that neatly folded into a mirrored case.

She opened the mirror and studied her face up close.

"Why do only your bottom teeth move when you chew?" she asked, as she watched herself in chewing motion.

I stopped, puzzled for a moment, and then slowly opened and closed my mouth several times. Sure enough, only my bottom teeth moved.

"I guess I never thought much about it," I admitted as I reached over and gave her an impulsive hug. That's when I noticed her hair. Obviously, she had invented the style just that morning—an uneven part down the middle with lots of barrettes in different places.

"Why don't you let me brush your hair, Kendall?"

"No!" she answered emphatically. "I like it this way."

"Okay," I shrugged, knowing that her confidence in her independence mattered greatly on this day.

I poured her a bowl of cereal and some milk, and she picked at it while she watched the clock.

"It's time," she finally squealed, quickly shoving her treasures into her backpack and dashing ahead of me out the door. I grabbed my camera as she skipped down the front steps.

We reached the end of our long driveway just as the huge yellow bus rounded the corner and lumbered to a stop with a squealing of brakes. I grabbed Kendall, hugged her tight, and then let her go.

"Bye, Mom!" she said, as she climbed up the steps.

I focused my camera, waiting to snap the picture as she turned around, but she didn't even look back. With a great whooshing sound, the doors closed and I took a picture of the bus pulling away. I couldn't even find Kendall's face among the noisy, laughing children in the windows.

I slowly started back down that long driveway toward a quiet house. I had planned to celebrate my freedom with a personal play day, but I didn't feel much like playing. I poured myself another cup of coffee and gazed out the window toward the range of Rocky Mountains across the valley.

With little prompting, memories started running through my mind. It's a funny thing about the seasons of life. While in the midst of one, especially the season of raising young children, the days crawl by, but as you look back on them, the years zoom by, like a video on a fast rewind.

As I sat there, I felt suspended in a strange, in-between place. I knew what I was leaving behind, but not yet what I was going to. So many good things were behind me. But what was in front of me? My sense of purpose, once clear, today seemed confused. And that familiar "Who am I?" question demanded a review. For the last season, mothering had been my primary description. But with all three children off in school, I needed to adjust my definition of what it meant to be a mother.

You see, mothering has a constantly changing job description—with planned obsolescence. The reality is, if I do it right, I work myself out of a job.

That's part of the predictable plan. And the way it should be. But on this day, the reality seemed hard to grasp. Or maybe I resisted.

How would I find firm footing on this shaky bridge of transition between two seasons?

At that moment, I had no clear answer.

Today, as I look back on that memorable time when Kendall went off to kindergarten, I see it as a pivotal moment typical of many of life's transitions. As life unfolds, we face many "letting go's," many good-byes at the end of long driveways, busy airports, or college dormitory parking lots. We face many seasonal changes that start with journeys across those wobbly bridges of transition. Through the years, I've become increasingly familiar with the footing on those bridges and less surprised by the emotions. And I'm more aware of how God gives us opportunities to begin shifting gears and preparing for those seasonal changes.

From my vantage point today, I see that our lives are made up of seasons that fit together in a predictable order, like wedges of a pie. I now accept these seasons as gifts from a God of order. As certainly as he gives us a predictable cycle of seasons in nature, he gives us a predictable cycle of seasons in our day-to-day lives.

And just as he provides signals of change in nature's seasons, such as frost on the pumpkin in the fall or brightly colored crocus poking through the blanket of snow in the spring, God also provides signals of change in the seasons of our lives. As our children grow up, they begin to show signs of increasing independence.

Walking across the school parking lot, a seven-year-old pulls her hand away as her mother automatically reaches for it. "Not here, Mom," she whispers.

Change is coming.

The adolescent spends more time in his room and a "Do Not Enter" sign appears on his closed door. "I need some privacy, Mom," he explains.

Change is coming.

College catalogues appear in the mailbox.

Change is coming.

Seasonal changes don't happen overnight; they come on slowly, giving us time to prepare. One way to prepare for those future changes is by relishing our time in the present. I learned this tip quite incidentally from a woman who was selling peaches at a roadside fruit stand as we were on our way home from delivering our two older ones to college several years ago.

For years, this annual late-summer trek to college campuses had doubled as a family vacation time, but this time Kendall stayed home because she didn't want to miss the first day of her junior year in high school. On the long drive back to Colorado, Lynn and I talked about the Empty Nest season ahead of us.

The more I anticipated that season, the deeper I sank into sadness. I knew I would grieve at the passing of the child-rearing era.

Just a few hours from home, we pulled into a fresh fruit stand on the western slope of the Colorado Rockies.

"The peaches are still great," the jovial lady behind the counter told us as she sliced into a fat, juicy peach and handed us each a piece.

We agreed, and tried to decide how many to buy.

"Get a whole bushel," she urged. "We're reaching the end of the season, and if you eat your fill now, you'll feel less regret when the season is over."

"She sounded like the Great Peach Philosopher," Lynn said as we drove away. I agreed, because the woman had shown me a truth about the change of seasons that transcended the world of peaches: If I seize upon and savor the ripe moments of the season I'm living, I'll have fewer regrets when that season ends.

I test-tried this attitude during Kendall's last two years of high school. I intentionally crossed nonessentials off my calendar so I would have more time and energy to attend almost all her basketball games and choir performances. I volunteered to drill her on Spanish vocabulary words at 10 P.M. and offered to go to the mall with her on some Saturday afternoons, one of my least favorite weekend activities.

By the time she left for college, I'd stuffed myself full of the "fruit of the season," so even though the season had ended, I had lots of memories and few regrets. I also had a better appetite of readiness for the next season.

There's something else about those memories I've been stuffing into my head and heart. I now see them as tangible reminders of God's unchanging character. He, who so richly blessed me in the past season, will surely continue to fill my life with blessings in the next season. In readiness, I have to open my eyes to see what he has in store for me.

I also have to let go of the past in order to make room for what the future holds. Even though the ending of a good season will leave me with some regrets, I have to remember that God, our Creator, always creates new beginnings out of endings. A new dawn out of the darkness of the night. The buds of springtime out of the dead of winter. As a new season emerges out of an ended one, I can anticipate new blessings, new challenges, new hopes.

God is a God of New Beginnings.

What about those difficult good-byes? I have to confess, I've never gotten much better about those. At the end of every Christmas vacation or summer vacation, during every drive to the airport or across the country to a college campus, I still get a tight throat and teary eyes. It's part of being a mom. I know that when we pour ourselves deeply into the lives of our children and love the way God calls us to love, good-byes will always be hard.

The truth is, love costs, and part of that cost is accepting pain as part of the joy that comes from loving another. But the pain also becomes part of the richness of our investment in relationships. Although we are not protected from the pain of change, our capacity to love can be enlarged by it. We learn to embrace others with greater sensitivity.

And finally, we can be comforted by a God who understands and knows that although good-byes and seasonal changes are difficult, they are part of the Master Plan that moves us closer to him.

Footprint Scripture

To every thing there is a season, and a time to every purpose under the heaven . . . (Ecc. 3:1 KJV).

Footprint Lessons

- God is a God of order. He gives us predictable seasons of life, just as he gives us predictable seasons in nature.

- God, who so richly blessed us in the last season, will richly bless us in the next season. His character does not change.

- The best way to prepare for the next season of life is to relish the one we are living in right now.

- Sometimes when seasons end, we have to say good-bye and let go. This can be painful. Yet pain becomes part of the joy of loving others the way God calls us to love. In our sadness, we are comforted by a God who understands our feelings.

- God, our Creator, creates something new out of something that is ending. He is the God of New Beginnings.

Reflections

1. Describe a change of seasons in your life—a change you have lived through or one you are anticipating. What is difficult about this change of seasons for you? What is good about it?

2. How are you preparing for the predictable changes of seasons ahead of you?

3. Did your parents adjust easily when you left home? What can you learn from how they handled their own changing seasons?

4. The pain we feel at times of separation or when saying good-bye is normal. Pain is part of the joy of loving another deeply. How do you respond to this thought?

part three

Facing Obstacles

. . . my power is made perfect in weakness.
2 Corinthians 12:9

Sometimes we come face-to-face with obstacles in our paths. Difficult circumstances that we don't understand. Feelings we can't shake. Fears that won't go away.

We stop and ask why, but we don't always get an answer. The "why" is one of the mysteries of life.

But still, we seek reasons or answers that make sense.

Finally, we reach the limits of our own strength. We realize we don't have the ability to control the future or change the circumstances or the feelings or the fears. In that stark moment, we have a choice: We can give up on God, or we can humbly surrender ourselves to him and rely on his strength in our weakness.

n i n e

Holding On and Letting Go

I'm a hopeless Fix-it Mom

As a new mother, I nervously confessed to the pediatrician that three-month-old Derek cried unless we rocked him to sleep.

The doctor, a gentle elderly man, smiled ever so slightly as he peered over the top of his glasses at me.

"You might let him cry himself to sleep a time or two," he casually suggested. "He'll learn."

It sounded like such a simple solution . . . until about two hours later when I put Derek down in his crib. Sure enough, he started to cry, and I began to endure the agony of listening to him.

In that next half hour, as I tried to ignore the sound of my child's periodic cries, I learned something about myself. It's a realization that became clearer to me over the next several years as we had a second child and then a third.

I am, instinctively and passionately, a Fix-it Mom.

I liked to fix crying spells by picking the baby up and rocking him. I liked to turn frowns upside down or set the neighborhood bully straight when he hurt my child's feelings. I liked to make life fair and fairly painless for my children.

I operated happily and almost obliviously in this Fix-it Mom mode until it came time to enroll Derek in preschool and the teacher invited parents to a preregistration meeting. I looked forward to learning more about the school that evening. Little did I know that I'd learn something much more valuable about being a mother.

"Welcome," the teacher warmly greeted us as we all perched precariously on preschool-sized chairs in the brightly decorated room.

"I have some forms for you to fill out, but I'd also like to talk to you about this step of independence your children are taking and tell you how you might help them. From my own experience, I know that parenting can bring out both the best and the worst in us," she continued kindly. "We love our children dearly and want to do things for them, but sometimes we *over*-love and *over*-do. We do things for them that they should be learning to do for themselves. The key is to find a balance between holding on and letting go as your children venture out into the world.

"Not everybody finds that balance easily. There are 'smother mothers,' who paralyze their children with dependence, and 'helicopter mothers,' who hover around anxiously and keep swooshing down to rescue their children whenever any difficulty approaches. These well-meaning moms do all the wrong things for all the right reasons. They over-protect out of their love for their children."

She closed her talk by challenging each of us to think about what we ultimately wanted for our children as they grew up.

"If you want your children to grow toward independence, consider how you might help them get to that place," the teacher urged. "Consider the character qualities you want them to acquire and then aim them toward those goals. You will be doing them—and yourselves—a favor. Now is the time to start."

As I sat there on my tiny chair, I felt as though the teacher was talking directly to me. I carried her advice home with me that night, along with a Fix-it Mom's prayer asking for God's help—help I knew I would surely need as I tried to apply this advice that went against the natural instincts of my heart to fix the world for my children.

Our children are almost adults now, and so often during their growing-up years, I have remembered back to what I learned in that preschool meeting long ago. Learning to let go is a challenge that creates a conflict between a mother's head and heart. In my head, I knew that kids learn in the midst of their struggles. But in my heart, I wanted to protect them from those struggles.

I also wanted to protect myself from the pain of watching and waiting while my kids discovered the lesson tucked into the struggle. While the baby cried himself to sleep. While the toddler kept falling down when learning to walk. While the preschooler struggled to find an appropriate response to another child who wouldn't share any toys.

I was, at times, tempted to rush in and rescue my children with a quick-fix solution. But I began to see that while quick fixes might feel good to me, they were not always the best solution for the child. In fact, my quick fixes could come between my children and their growth toward independence.

Someone once said that the process of parenting is a lot like teaching a child to ride a two-wheeled bicycle. The parent runs alongside and holds on while the child gets the hang of it. But the parent knows that the ultimate goal is for the child to learn to maneuver around the obstacles in the path with confidence, alone. So eventually a parent has to let go, even though that parent knows the child will wobble around and fall down a few times while learning.

Like Derek's preschool teacher said, we need to identify what we ultimately want for our children and then keep aiming them toward it. If we want them to become confident and capable, we have to step back and give them the opportunity to learn.

In stepping aside, we also get an opportunity to trust that God cares for our children even more than we do. And that, ultimately, he is shaping them for his purposes.

I found lots of those opportunities for growth and trust while our kids were growing up.

One happened about six years after my preschool parenting lesson. Derek was nine years old, and I had stopped to pick him up at the pool after swim team practice one hot summer morning.

"Mom," he grabbed my arm, "I got in trouble." With those words, the tears he'd been holding back welled up in his eyes.

"The lifeguard . . ." he tried to take a deep breath and piece the story together . . . "she blamed me . . . I was trying to help Hillary get her dolls back from the kids who took them to tease her. . . ."

Another deep breath.

"The lifeguard saw me with the dolls and blamed me for taking them," he sputtered, now rubbing his eyes with a fist to hide his tears so his friends wouldn't see him crying. "She got mad at me in front of everyone. It wasn't fair, Mom," he cried, looking up at me pleadingly.

It didn't seem fair. Derek thought he was helping a friend, and got blamed for something he didn't do by someone who (according to Derek) jumped to the wrong conclusion and embarrassed him.

As I put my arm around him, I felt that familiar urge to rise up and quickly fix the situation. I felt the familiar struggle between my head and my heart. But I paused and thought about my greater responsibility to Derek—the ultimate, long-range goal.

"Derek," I suggested, "I understand you are hurt, because it sounds like the lifeguard made a mistake. I'll be glad to go with you if you'd like to talk to her and explain what happened."

"No," he said firmly. "I want to go home."

"Okay, then let's get your towel and go. "

More than anything, I wanted to march right over and tell that lifeguard she had hurt my son's feelings. I wanted to fix his hurt and settle the unfairness. But more important, I knew Derek would learn nothing if I simply removed the obstacle while he sat down and watched. He needed to learn to maneuver around these obstacles himself, because I wouldn't always be there to run alongside or take them out of his way.

The Bible gives a powerful example of this model of parenting in the way that Jesus teaches his disciples. The disciples faced many storms in life, both figuratively and physically. Often they found themselves crossing the Sea of Galilee, known for its fierce waves and sudden storms. Once, when Jesus was sleeping in the boat while the disciples battled a frightening storm, they woke him and he quickly calmed the waters—he fixed the circumstances. But later, as they matured and faced similar storms, Jesus waited on shore and watched them struggle. Sometimes, instead of changing or fixing the circumstances, he changed the disciples themselves as they learned to cope in the midst of the storm.

I still have to keep reminding myself of that lesson.

For instance, one night recently, Kendall called long-distance from her college dormitory. She was feeling discouraged. She'd had a misunderstanding with a friend; a professor had set an unfair deadline for a paper, and her bank account balance seemed incorrectly low. Immediately I wanted to send money, criticize both the professor and her friend, and fix all her problems.

My instinctive, protective response reminded me that there is some bad news and some good news about the lifelong challenge of learning to let go.

The bad news is that a Fix-it Mom never outgrows her desire to fix the circumstances and make life less painful for her children. Even her grown children.

The good news is that a Fix-it Mom can improve her ability to recognize when to step in and when to step back. She can realize that her duty is not to fix the world for her children, but to fix her children to learn to cope in the world.

"I'm praying for you, Kendall," I told her over the phone that night. And when I hung up, I imagined her wobbling away and gaining confidence on that two-wheeled bicycle called life.

Footprint Scripture

Perseverance must finish its work so that you may be mature and complete, not lacking anything (James 1:4).

Footprint Lessons

- Learning to let go presents a conflict between our heads and our hearts. Instinctively we want to hold on and protect our children, but ultimately our goal is let go and allow them to grow toward independence.

- Letting go is the slow, orderly process of transferring freedom and responsibility, year by year, as our children grow up, so that by the time they leave home, they will be confident and capable of making appropriate choices and coping in the world.

- Letting go is like teaching a child to ride a two-wheeler. We run alongside and hold on while they get the hang of it, and then we let them wobble off alone. Even if they fall down a few times, the goal is to let them learn to maneuver on their own.

- A parent's responsibility is not to clear the path of obstacles but to step out of the way and allow the child to learn to cope with the obstacles.

- Fix-it Moms have to trust God in the process of letting go. We have to trust that he cares for our children, and that he is, ultimately, shaping them for his purposes.

Reflections

1. In what ways are you holding on instead of letting go of your children?

2. What are your goals for your children? Start with the end in mind. What qualities do you want them to acquire as they grow up?

3. How are you intentionally helping them reach those goals and acquire these qualities?

4. What are some of the challenges you are allowing your children to face?

5. If you are still running alongside that bicycle, why are you afraid of letting your children wobble off alone?

ten

A Sick Child

*What happens
when there is no cure?*

If you asked me about my single greatest fear in life, it is that something might happen to one of my children. Something life-altering or life-threatening. Something I couldn't change or fix.

The day I faced that fear is the day I learned how to cope with it.

It all started on a perfectly normal Saturday night.

We thought nine-year-old Derek had the flu, so I made him a bed of fluffy comforters on the floor next to our bed, the spot where sick children in our family get to spend the night. Derek kept throwing up all night long, and I knew by morning that I had to call the doctor. Derek looked frighteningly gaunt, with sunken eyes. He whimpered for something to drink, but even sucking an ice cube made him sick all over again.

When the pediatrician finally returned my call, he asked a few questions and then advised me to bring Derek to his office. Lynn and the two younger girls went off to Sunday school, and Derek and I headed for the doctor's office.

By the time we got there, Derek seemed nearly unconscious. The doctor met us at the door and ushered us into an examining room, where he took a couple of tests and then left us alone while he went down the hall to check the results. His footsteps echoed eerily in the quiet office. In a few moments, he returned.

"We have juvenile diabetes here," he announced quietly, looking down at Derek, who lay crumpled into a heap on the examining table. "You need to get him to the hospital right away to get him on an IV."

His next words grew muffled as the room kind of swirled around me.

Diabetes. The word conjured up pictures of frail, sickly children . . . of my husband's cousin who died of the disease in his twenties. The word had nothing to do with this normally healthy, athletic child.

"Be strong for Derek," I told myself as I helped him back into the car while trying to blink back the tears that burned at the corners of my eyes. Derek seemed too lethargic to notice.

As I rushed to the hospital, a million fears zoomed through my mind.

How could this be? I thought Derek had the flu and the doctor would give us some medicine to make him well. But this time there was no prescription and no medicine. This time, there was no cure.

Lynn soon joined me at the hospital and, while Derek slept, we listened as the doctor explained that Derek's pancreas no longer produced sufficient insulin to meet his body's needs. He now would have to take insulin injections at least twice a day and follow a strict diet, carefully balancing his food intake with regular exercise.

We would have to monitor his blood sugar levels with daily blood and urine tests, and learn to detect and deal with the inevitable insulin reactions. Yet in spite of these precautions, Derek could still face frightening complications that could change and even threaten his life.

The information seemed overwhelming.

That afternoon, I wandered alone up and down the halls of the hospital, trying to imagine Derek's future. No longer would he have the freedom to run out the door and play without thinking of the supplies he needed; no longer could he go to a birthday party and eat cake and ice cream. It seemed as if his carefree childhood had died in a matter of hours.

I found a quiet, dark stairwell, where I sat down and cried out my tears of grief.

Later that night, Lynn and I sat by Derek's bed in the dimly lit hospital room, holding hands and talking about the events of the day. We ached as we gazed at our sleeping child, an IV tube running into his body. We felt so helpless. For the first time in our lives, we were keenly aware of our inability to control our child's future.

"I think we should pray," Lynn finally said.

And then, in halting sentences uttered by both of us, we said this prayer:

"Lord, in the past we've had trouble believing that you love our children more than we do and that you will take care of them. We've assumed that we can control their lives. For the first time, we face a health problem with no human solution. We can't cure it or change it. So we come to you—in humble dependence—and place this child in your hands. We surrender him to you. We know you have a plan for his life. Please take care of him. And help us to accept your plan for him with trust and loving support."

We didn't know what Derek's future held, but we knew that facing it started with this total surrender. Still, I felt afraid.

Derek is now twenty-four years old, and as I look back upon that crisis when I faced what I thought was the worst fear of my life, I realize I took a great step of growth in my faith. For Derek's diabetes made me recognize my helplessness, which forced me to a place of surrender and total dependence upon God.

There is no safer place.

I've often heard people talk about a moment when they reach the end of themselves—the end of their adequacy, of the limit of their strength or ability to control their future or the future of a loved one. At that moment they have a choice. They can give up and turn their backs on God, or they can turn to God and surrender that unknown future to him.

It can be a holy moment.

In our case, we had to surrender our child's uncertain future. I didn't know then that God has given us a model of this parental surrender. It is the story of Abraham, in the book of Genesis in the Bible, who trudges up Mt. Moriah to surrender his son to God. In that journey, Abraham learned that when we surrender our children to God, he provides—for them and for us.

Abraham was old when he and Sara had their baby boy, Isaac. How they must have longed for this child and planned their dreams around his future, even before the child was born. I can only imagine the love Abraham must have felt the first time he stooped down to cradle that precious bundle in his arms. No wonder that, as the boy grew, they bonded closely and Isaac became the treasure of his father's heart. Maybe Abraham even began treasuring Isaac more than he trusted God. Maybe unknowingly, he began to put the boy first in his heart. Sometimes parents do that. Sometimes I do that.

For whatever reason, God tested Abraham. The test was actually one of whether Abraham trusted God. God told Abraham to take Isaac up Mt. Moriah and surrender him there as a sacrifice to God.

Surely Abraham did not understand why Isaac had to face these difficult circumstances. Surely he felt filled with fear about the boy's uncertain future. Yet Abraham knew he was not in control of his son's future. God was. He knew God loved his son even more than Abraham did, and that ultimately, God had a plan for his son's life. And for Abraham's life. And that plan was bigger than these current circumstances.

Abraham knew he had to surrender the treasure of his heart to God.

So he trudged all the way to the top of the mountain, to the place of total surrender. But just when it seemed the boy would die, God provided a substitute sacrifice—a ram caught in the thicket nearby. Only then did Abraham realize that when a parent surrenders a child to God in total trust, God provides. In his way. In his time.

Abraham called that mountain "Jehovah Jireh," which means "God will provide." And that promise still echoes down from that ancient place to all of us who surrender our children to God in trust.

That journey up Mt. Moriah is, for all parents, a symbolic journey of surrender. It does not happen on a physical mountain, but in the attitude of our hearts when we relinquish the treasure of our hearts to God in trust. It is a journey I've taken over and over again as our children have grown up and faced circumstances beyond my control.

I've learned that this surrender is more than a resigned acceptance of some difficult, uncontrollable circumstances. Instead, it is a relinquishment we come to by hoping and trusting in God, in his faithfulness, and in his promise that he will provide in the face of circumstances we don't understand. Or can't control. Like diabetes.

In Derek's case, I have accumulated a long list of the ways in which God has provided since that prayer of total surrender in the hospital. He provided courage for all of us when we left a tearful ten-year-old boy at a camp for diabetic children because the doctor recommended that a week away would help him learn to take care of himself. He provided Derek with the kind of personality that accepts the strict discipline of his diabetic condition. He provided an understanding roommate when Derek went off to college and faced some frightening diabetic reactions. And most important, he has provided the perfect pathway that has shaped Derek and given him a sensitivity for other kids in need, which has led him into a ministry of helping troubled adolescents.

I looked my worst fear in the face that day at the hospital. Though I feared what Derek's future might hold, I can see how God has provided mightily for Derek after our prayer of surrender.

We still don't know what Derek's future holds, but we know who holds that future. And we know that God will provide. And be sufficient. And work all things together for good.

Footprint Scripture

And we know that in all things God works for the good of those who love him, who have been called according to his purpose (Rom. 8:28).

Footprint Lessons

- When we look our worst fear in the face and turn to God, we learn that God is sufficient.

- God promises that when we surrender a child to him, he will provide strength to meet our challenges.

- The act of surrendering is a conscious, intentional choice. It is more than the resigned acceptance of difficult circumstances; it is a relinquishment with hope and trust in the character of God.

- When we reach a place of helplessness, we can either turn our backs on God or turn towards him. Helplessness can draw us near to God in a holy moment, as we reach the end of our own ability to handle things.

- God does weave all of our circumstances together for good, just as he promises. In his time. In his way. When we trust him.

Reflections

1. Do you remember a moment—or an experience—when you reached the "end of yourself" and recognized that you could not control your future or your child's future? How did you respond?

2. Read the account of Abraham and Isaac in Genesis 22. Why did God "test" Abraham's trust?

3. What does it mean "to surrender your child to God"?

4. How has God shown you the evidence of his promise that "the Lord will provide" when we surrender to him?

5. What helps you to believe his promise . . . or keeps you from believing his promise?

e l e v e n

Down Days

Sometimes I don't know how to keep going

A simple, single sentence announcement on the radio turned my day upside down.

"Boulder Valley Schools will be closed today due to the overnight blizzard."

"Oh no," I moaned, pulling the covers over my head.

With that announcement at 6 A.M., my three children received the delightful gift of an unexpected holiday. And I received the unexpected assignment of a day on indoor duty on the front lines of motherhood.

It's not what I had planned for this day.

I had planned to get the two older ones off on the bus, quickly clean the house, drop Kendall off at preschool, and then spend the rest of the quiet morning finishing a writing project for my part-time job.

I crawled out of bed and opened the curtains. Sure enough, large fluffy snow flakes swirled outside our window. Lynn got up, checked the amount of snow in the driveway, and decided he could make it to his office. By 7 A.M. he was gone, and the day stretched endlessly before me.

Soon the kids were up, squealing with delight at the surprise of a free play day.

"Let's make pancakes," Lindsay suggested enthusiastically. "The picture kind."

"Okay," I agreed, vowing to get into their mood. So I heated up the griddle, mixed up the batter, and began pouring the "pictures." Three connected plops for a snowman, numbers for each of their ages, and three misshapen hearts.

"Make a bicycle," Derek begged.

"No way," I objected.

"Then let me try."

He did, dribbling the batter all the way across the stovetop.

"There!" he said proudly, looking at the glob on the griddle.

With breakfast over, the kids started their cycle of going outside and coming back inside. "Outside" meant zipping them into heavy coats, pulling on their boots and mittens, and sending them out the door. "Inside" meant welcoming them back in, pulling off their snowy boots and soggy mittens and wet coats that left puddles on the floor. Our deliriously happy dog followed them in and out, bounding through the house, leaving chunks of melting snow all over the carpet.

In between the "in" and "out," cups of hot chocolate were requested and then left half-finished and sticky on the counter. By midmorning, the house smelled like a mixture of wet wool, pancake syrup, and chocolate.

We tried making cookies, which started out as a good idea but turned into a bad idea when three-year-old Kendall spilled a cup of flour into the silverware drawer.

"Sorry, Mom, it was *on accident!*" (Which is the opposite of *on purpose.*)

After baking two batches, I ended up letting them eat the remaining cookie dough, just to finish off the project more quickly.

By noon, the walls of the house began closing in on all of us. I was running out of enthusiasm and concerned about the writing project I needed to finish, and the kids were starting to pick on each other.

"She looked at me, Mom," one complained.

"Is that a problem?" I asked.

"I don't like her to look at me. Make her stop looking at me."

I knew we needed another diversion. "Let's make a blanket fort in the living room," I suggested. Blanket forts were one of their favorite indoor pastimes.

"Yeah!" they yelled in unison, as they scattered to pull blankets and comforters out of closets and off beds. I then helped them pin several blanket corners to couches and chairs, and anchored a few more with piles of books on top of tables. Soon the room was transformed into a maze of dark secret hiding places.

"Can we have a picnic in here?" Lindsay asked.

"Sure, I'll bring you some sandwiches."

A few minutes later they were scrunched together in a small place between the couch and the coffee table, eating peanut butter and jelly sandwiches and telling scary stories.

"It's dark in here," I heard Kendall say quietly.

"Don't worry, silly," her older sister told her. "You know it's light outside."

They seemed contented, so I retreated to a comfy chair by the window in our bedroom, where I watched the storm still piling up the snow outside the window.

It was only 1 P.M., and I'd hit the no-school-snow-day slump, that moment when you realize you have run out of juice before the day has run out of hours. The darkness of depression began to descend upon me, yet I knew I had to keep going.

It wasn't one single thing that caused this dark mood, but the nebulous accumulation of many things. A day's plans gone awry. The lack of feeling of accomplishment. The monotony of wiping off sticky kitchen counters. The fear that I might never do anything but maintenance chores for the rest of my life. The fatigue. The discouragement.

I felt like I was in a room where someone kept dimming the light, finally leaving me in darkness. I felt like Kendall in the blanket fort.

How does a mom get through a dark slump on a no-school snow day?

Just recently, there was another no-school snow day. I heard the announcement on the radio when I woke up, and felt a bit nostalgic because there are no longer any kids at home to squeal with delight at the news of an unexpected holiday. But I vividly remember the personality of those days, and many others like them, when a mom runs out of energy and a dark mood of depression starts to descend and choke out all the light.

The longer I live, the less surprised I am by those down days, when God feels far away and I feel sad or discouraged. A lot of life requires us to carry on in the midst of days that don't feel good. To keep doing things we don't feel like doing. To keep on keeping on.

But I've learned that life is not based on our feelings so much as faith in the facts. And here's a fact: Snow storms and slumps and dark days are temporary. They come, but they will go.

When I remember back to my no-school-snow-day slump, I realize that the clouds lifted the next day. The sun returned, the snow started to melt, and my slump disappeared. In God's pattern of days, storms and slumps and dark times are temporary. So many of God's promises point to this truth. When we believe those promises, we can endure in those dark places with less resistance.

Here's another fact: God wants us to discover some truths about him in those dark places. Just the other day, twenty-three-year-old Lindsay called me long-distance. She was having a down day. She has just graduated from college, moved to a new city, and is looking for a job. She hasn't yet found a circle of new friends. This particular day, she was feeling lonely and several discouragements were piling up around her.

"God has something for you in this down day," I found myself telling her. "Consider it like a place that you are in just for today, like those blanket forts you used to build in the living room. You won't stay in that place, so while you're there, fully explore it. Embrace it. Treat it like a temporary adventure. Examine the corners. Sit quietly in the darkness. Look for what is there for you. It may enrich you and help you reach out to others in the future. It may help you trust what you know about God.

"Remember what you used to tell Kendall when she got tired of the darkness in those blanket forts: *Don't worry, silly. You know it's light outside.*"

A few days later, Lindsay called back. She was closing in on a couple of great job possibilities. She'd made a friend. The down day was past history.

This brings up yet another fact: When we're in a dark or down place, God wants us to remember what we learned in the light.

A ten-year-old boy helped me learn this truth a few years ago.

He was exploring an abandoned mine with his father when the two got separated. The father felt horrified when he realized his son was not at his side and more horrified when his calls couldn't locate the boy. Soon a full-fledged search party entered the mine and began looking, but the mine was so blackly dark that they literally could not see their hands in front of their faces.

For three days search parties combed that mine, and on the fourth day, they gave up hope. No child could survive that long. They decided to blast a rock across the entry to the mine to seal it shut so no other child would ever face that same horrifying experience. Just before they did, a man who knew the mine succeeded in convincing the authorities he had a hunch where the child might be, so they let him go in for one last search. Sure enough, he found the boy alive, deep down inside the mine in the pocket of a small tunnel.

How did the child survive?

"I knew I wasn't alone," the little boy said. "I knew God was with me, and I knew someone would come get me, so I went to sleep."

The boy's faith allowed him to sleep peacefully the entire time, even in that dark place, and that calm sleep saved his life. It slowed down his metabolism so he was able to survive. He remembered in the dark what he learned in the light.

That's the same message that Lindsay passed on to Kendall in the blanket fort. *Don't worry, silly. You know it's light outside.* As we grow older, we have to remember these messages of child-like faith and truth that sustain us and carry us through the dark or down days.

Because down days don't last. But God's promises do.

Footprint Scripture

God turns my darkness into light . . .(Ps. 18:28).

Footprint Lessons

- In the pattern of life, we have good days and not-so-good days; sunny days and dark days. This up-and-down pattern is normal. A lot of life simply requires that we keep on keeping on.

- Dark, down days don't last. Storms pass. Clouds disappear. The sunshine returns. Many of God's promises point to this truth.

- God has something for us, even in a down day. When you feel down, look around. Treat it like a temporary adventure. Ask what God wants you to learn in this moment.

- Our ability to persevere on a down day is not based on our feelings so much as our faith in the facts of God's promises.

- God wants us to remember in the dark what we learned in the light.

Reflections

1. Describe a recent down day.

2. What do you learn from a down day?

3. What does the sentence "Remember in the dark what you learned in the light" mean to you?

4. How can you apply "putting your faith in facts, not feelings" to your life?

5. What advice would you give someone else when they are experiencing a down day?

twelve

Worrying

It's part of a mother's job description

"Mom, you worry too much," my ten-year-old daughter Lindsay told me as we prepared to leave our house early one summer Saturday morning.

I hate it when that happens: My own child makes a critical observation about me, and I know she is absolutely right. I do worry too much, but I've always rationalized that worrying is an important part of a mother's job description. In fact, it's something I do well. And why not? I get plenty of practice!

I started worrying almost from the moment I discovered I was pregnant. I began worrying whether I'd taken any harmful medicine before I knew I was pregnant; whether each of my babies would be born healthy; and whether I could make it through each delivery without drugs.

With each of my children's births, I discovered a whole new supply of legitimate worries—like whether they were still breathing in the middle of the night, or getting enough breast milk, or becoming spoiled as they recognized their power to manipulate me with their cries. My supply of worries was fueled by frightening stories I read or heard about toddlers drinking cleaning fluids or falling down manholes or choking on cookies or pieces of toys. My own mother warned me not to use booties with strings because of some story she'd heard.

No wonder that by the time Lindsay reached the age of ten, she knew I worried too much. But on the particular morning she made that observation, I had plenty of good reasons to worry. For the first time, we were hitching our car up to our new horse trailer, loading her horse onto it, and driving twenty miles down a busy road to the county fairgrounds for a 4-H horse show. Lynn was out of town, so it was just Lindsay and me. The mere thought of it gave me a headfull of worries about the possible dangers.

First of all, horses worried me. They weigh about twelve hundred pounds, wear sharp steel shoes on all four feet, and sometimes rear up, like in the old-time cowboy movies. I often wondered why, out of all the possibilities, God gave me a daughter with a passion for horses. Why not ballet or soccer or reading? Some safe activity where I could drop her off at the local recreation center for a lesson, run to the grocery store, and pick her up later?

But Lindsay loved horses. And since we lived on four acres in the country . . . and since someone in the neighborhood was practically giving a horse away . . . and since everybody knows 4-H is good for kids, here we were on this summer morning, hitching the horse trailer up to the car.

That was another thing that presented a worry. Though I'd practiced driving the trailer around the neighborhood, I'd never driven the rig down a real highway, through busy intersections, in real traffic, with a real horse inside. I'd heard horror stories about trailers coming unhitched or horses tipping over inside the trailer and falling out the back door.

Now I know I'm supposed to give my worries to God, and I tried, but they didn't disappear; they continued to roll around and grow bigger inside my head. Still, I knew I couldn't back out of this adventure. Lindsay had looked forward to this horse show for weeks.

So we carefully hooked the horse trailer up to the car, checked all the little nuts and bolts on the hitch, and then Lindsay calmly loaded up her horse. I slammed and bolted the back door and then double- and triple-checked it. And checked the hitch again.

"Are you sure the horse is okay?" I asked Lindsay.

That's when she rolled her eyes and told me I worried too much.

I said a silent prayer as we climbed into the car, and we slowly inched our way down the driveway and out onto the highway.

"Isn't this great?" Lindsay asked excitedly. But when we didn't speed up, she looked at me kind of strangely and said, "What's wrong, Mom?"

"Nothing. Why?" I asked a bit defensively.

"We can't go this slow all the way to the fairgrounds."

"Why not?" But again I knew she was right, so I picked up a little speed . . . until I saw the first stoplight a couple of blocks ahead. Lindsay rolled her eyes again as I began slowing down. As we turned the first corner, I felt the horse shift, but he didn't tip over or fall out the back. As we neared the railroad tracks, Lindsay reminded me of what I already knew.

"This is the place where the Bakers' trailer came unhitched last year."

My heart nearly stopped, and I gripped the wheel tighter as we bumped across the tracks, but nothing happened.

I continued to worry my way all the way to the fairgrounds, and felt so relieved when we finally got there that I pulled into a spot right up against the barn.

"We made it!" I announced to Lindsay with a grin.

Then suddenly, a whole new worry hit me.

I was smack dab up against that barn, and I had no idea how to back up the doggone trailer!

Worrying is a habit not easily broken.

Yet as I look back upon the development of the worry-habit in my life, I also see some steps of progress in dealing with it. My horse trailering days were pivotal in that process, because I started to learn what to do with my worries when I hitched up that trailer, and I've been trying to practice ever since.

It was during those days that I found a story in the Bible about a mother who had lots of reasons to worry. Her name was Jochebed, an Israelite who had a baby named Moses. During this time in Egypt, Pharaoh, the Egyptian ruler, wanted to control the growing number of Israelites, so he demanded all the newborn Israelite boys be killed. For three months, Jochebed hid her newborn son. And then she made a plan. She got a basket and carefully prepared it to hold her baby. She placed baby Moses in it and then floated the basket down the Nile River, where he was rescued and eventually raised by Pharaoh's own daughter.

Out of a head-full of worries, this mother picked out the ones she could control and surrendered the rest to God. She did the possible, and left the impossible to him. By her actions, she showed me a formula I began to use when dealing with my worries.

When my head started filling up with worries about driving the horse trailer, I imagined myself dumping them all out on a table and then separating out the ones I could control from the ones I couldn't control. It was within my control to check the hitch and the latches on the doors and to drive carefully. But after doing what I could do, I had to turn the things I couldn't control into a prayer and give them to God.

This same idea is behind the message of the well-known Serenity Prayer:

> *God grant me the serenity*
> *to accept the things I cannot change,*
> *the courage to change the things I can,*
> *and the wisdom to know the difference.*

Reinhold Niebuhr

I realized I had made some progress in my habit of worrying when I faced a challenge which reminded me of my horse trailering days. In this more recent experience, Lindsay and I again sat side by side in the front seat of a car. We didn't have a horse trailer hitched on behind, but this time Lindsay sat behind the wheel of the car and I sat on the passenger side.

She was learning to drive, and I was teaching her.

Again, I had a head-full of worries about possible dangers. For one thing, Lindsay approached the challenge of driving the same way she approached life as a teenager: fearlessly. I approached the challenge of teaching her to drive the same way I approached life as the mother of a teenager: fearfully. There is something distinctly unsettling about looking over and realizing that the person behind the wheel is the same girl-child who, only yesterday it seems, drove the bumper cars at the amusement park and delighted in whamming into everybody in sight.

On this particular day, I had picked her up at her high school.

After throwing her books in the backseat, she climbed in behind the wheel, waved to some friends, and popped the car into reverse.

As we shot backwards, I slapped my hands on the dashboard to brace myself, and that's when I got the familiar "Mom, you worry too much," along with the rolled eyes. Then she added, "You know that when you worry, you make me worry."

Again, I knew she was right. My worries took away her confidence. So I busied myself with tightening my seat belt and practicing the same deep breathing techniques that helped me relax during labor pains when she was born. The breathing helped distract me from the worries.

We pulled out of the parking lot and headed down a small hill toward an intersection.

"Be careful!" Once again I slapped my hands on the dashboard as Lindsay slammed on the brakes in the middle of the intersection.

"What's wrong?" she asked.

"You can't assume others are watching out for you at intersections. You have to drive defensively." Again she rolled her eyes and I went back to my breathing exercises.

By the time we turned into our driveway, I reminded myself of the mother in the cartoon I had taped to our refrigerator door. In it, a smiling teenager is climbing out from behind the wheel of the car. "Thanks for the lesson, Mom!" she says. Meanwhile, the mother is seated on the passenger side with a look of terror frozen on her face . . . and her feet thrust right through the floorboards of the car.

I also reminded myself of the worrywart mother I used to be, worrying my way all the way to the fairgrounds with the horse trailer, before I started using the Jochebed formula for dealing with worries. It was time to go back to the formula.

I had to imagine myself dumping out all my worries about teaching Lindsay to drive and then picking out the ones I could control. I could control the amount of driving experience she got in the next few weeks before she turned sixteen and got her license. I could take her to shopping mall parking lots, freeway on-ramps, busy highways, and slippery streets. I could give her confidence by controlling my worries in front of her. I could make sure we had a safe car for her to drive. And after I picked out the parts I could control, I had to surrender the rest to God.

On Lindsay's sixteenth birthday, she took the driving test and passed easily. Then she dropped me off at home and asked if she could take the car to a friend's house.

Alone.

Even though my head started filling with those "what-if" worries, I agreed.

As I watched her pull out of the driveway, I remembered Jochebed. Sure, there were worrisome things out there on those highways. Yes, accidents do happen. But I'd done what I could do, and now she was out of my hands.

It was time to turn the rest of my worries into a prayer and give them over to God.

Footprint Scripture

*Do not be anxious about anything, but in every-
thing, by prayer and petition, with thanksgiving,
present your requests to God. And the peace of
God, which transcends all understanding, will
guard your hearts and your minds in Christ Jesus
(Phil. 4:6–7).*

Footprint Lessons

- Worrying is a bad habit we can break.

- Worrying is taking on a responsibility that belongs
to God.

- When your head fills with worries, stop. Dump all the
worries out on a table, pick out the ones you can control, then turn the leftovers into a prayer and give them
to God.

- When you are sorting through your worries, remember
the Serenity Prayer. We need to determine what is possible and surrender the impossible to God.

- When parents worry out loud, we pass our worries on to
our children.

Reflections

1. What worries are filling your head today?

2. Imagine yourself laying those worries out on a table. Make a plan for each of the worries you can control.

3. What worries are left over? How can you turn those into a prayer to God?

4. Read the story of Jochebed (Ex. 2). As a mother, how might you feel in those circumstances?

5. What is God teaching you about dealing with your worries? How can you apply the above footprint Scripture to your life today?

thirteen

A Dying Friend

I'm afraid . . .

My phone rang midmorning one Saturday. It was my good friend Lois.

"I've just gotten back from the doctor's office," she told me quietly. "I have inoperable lung cancer."

Stunned, I tried to make sense of her words. Then I reacted.

"Lois, this can't be! You're healthy. You're only forty-two years old. You've never smoked. This doesn't make sense."

I wanted to rationalize away her horrible news.

"I know," she said softly, and I could tell she was crying.

"I'll be right there," I told her.

After I hung up, I sat on my bed and angrily punched my fist into a pillow. Then I said a prayer: *Lord, please heal Lois, and give me the strength to walk alongside her wherever this journey takes us. Don't let my fears get in the way of helping her.*

I grabbed my purse and car keys, and found thirteen-year-old Lindsay in the kitchen eating cereal.

"I'm going to see Lois," I told her. "I'll be back within an hour."

With that, I got in the car and drove to Lois' house, where we cried together.

Lois and I had been friends since our teenagers were babies together, her two and my three. We met on a tennis court, where I was immediately drawn by her mixture of honesty, determination, and humor. Soon our friendship grew beyond our common interest in tennis.

We often traded kids and shared our parenting struggles, from dealing with picky eaters to picking out the best preschools. When she became a single parent after a difficult divorce, I was there. When my mother died, she was there. Several years later, when she remarried a wonderful man named Don, I brought the punch bowl and helped host her backyard reception.

Now I needed to be there for her in a whole new way.

In the beginning, Lois admitted her "what-if" fears about what might be ahead as she started her chemotherapy treatments. "What if I lose all my hair?" she asked one day, as she ran her fingers through her thick dark hair. "What if I get too weak to take a walk . . . or have to stay in bed all the time?" she asked as we strolled on a pathway through her neighborhood. "What if Don gets tired of caring for me? What if I'm not around when my children need me?"

Each fear seemed bigger than the last.

I didn't have many good answers, but I got her a whimsical tennis hat to cover up her thinning hair and had "Lois' Lid" embroidered in bright green on the brim. I told her I'd rig up a giant slingshot to catapult her out of bed if she got too weak. I especially understood her fear about not being there for her children, so I promised that I would try to stay close to them, no matter what happened. Mostly, I listened to her and hoped she couldn't tell that the thought of her dying made me feel afraid too.

In spite of the chemotherapy, her cancer progressed. But even though Lois got weaker, her faith grew stronger, and she seemed less fearful and more peaceful as time went on. When she lost all her hair, she modeled one of her new wigs.

"I kind of like these curls for a change," she grinned.

When she could no longer walk around the neighborhood, she seemed content to let me push her in a wheelchair, which we dubbed "Her Royal Carriage." And when she had to carry a canister of oxygen, it became "O–2," like a friendly companion out of a science fiction movie. On one of our walks, we passed a pond where a mother duck tended to her babies.

"I now know," Lois told me with confidence, "that God will not take me to heaven unless he intends to provide for my children."

One drizzly spring morning a few months later, she called to ask if I would stop by.

"What's up?" I asked when I found her seated at her kitchen table, surrounded by some papers and a bright red folder.

"I'm finishing some tasks today and hope you're strong enough to help me. I'm planning my memorial service, and I'd like you to do the eulogy."

A bolt of fear shot through me.

"I'm not sure I can handle that," I stammered.

"Of course you can," she went on, without a pause, as if the matter was settled. "I want this to be a celebration of joy and hope. Don't make me out to be a saint, and here's a list of my favorite Scriptures and songs." She shoved the papers back into the red folder and handed it to me. "And thanks," she added softly with the slightest catch in her voice. "I don't want Don to have to deal with this."

I took the red folder and gave her a hug, without admitting I couldn't imagine standing up in front of people and talking about her some day in the future after she died. It seemed a fearful impossibility.

Finally the day came when Lois could no longer get out of bed. Her parents came from California. Don took more time off work, and we all took turns sitting by her bed.

The last time I saw Lois, I moistened her parched lips with a swab of cotton, recited some of her favorite Bible verses, and gently told her that she had walked this journey with faith and courage. I didn't know if she could hear me.

Without opening her eyes, she reached up and touched my face.

"You've done good too," she whispered. "Thanks."

Lois died two days later.

Though I had expected her death, I struggled with the reality of it. I had a hard time connecting the word "death" with Lois. And I struggled with the fearful thought of fulfilling my promise to give the eulogy at her memorial service.

I prayed for strength. I walked around her neighborhood on the paths we'd often taken together and remembered our conversations. Her fears. Her faith. Her peace. I examined the contents of her red folder, read her favorite Scriptures, and jotted a few notes down on a piece of paper.

Two days later, I sat in the church, clutching my crumpled page of notes, waiting for Lois' service to start. My stomach felt queasy and my head felt hot. Could I deliver this message? Finally it was time, and I stood up.

"Hello," I said as I faced a mass of faces. "I want to tell you about our friend, Lois, and her courageous journey toward heaven in this last year . . ."

I don't really remember what I said, but somehow I got through her eulogy. I didn't cry. In fact, the most amazing thing happened. I didn't even feel afraid. When I got right up to doing what I feared, the fear disappeared. Like a mirage.

Is that what happened to Lois as she faced her fears? I wondered.

Recently, I had lunch with Lois' daughter, Melinda, who is about to graduate from college. Every time she comes back to Boulder, we get together. She calls herself my "other daughter," a title I like, because it reminds me of my vow to Lois that I would stay close to her children.

We talked about what Melinda would do after college and her normal fears about the unknowns in her future.

"Your mom taught me lots about facing fears in the future," I told Melinda. "A fear is a feeling about something that *might* happen tomorrow or next week or next year. As you stand on the moment of today and look ahead to that place, you feel afraid because you're imagining that possibility. And you're imagining how you'll feel if that happens. But you don't know how God will prepare you or change your heart or provide for you when you get there.

"When your mom first got the news of her cancer, she looked at the possibilities ahead of her and felt afraid. But when she reached each of those places she feared, God provided the strength she needed. She feared losing her hair and losing her physical vitality, but when both of those things happened, they no longer mattered. She greatly feared the thought of leaving Don and you two kids, but slowly her trust grew in God's promises that he would provide for you. When she got right up to the edge of what she feared, God transformed her fears into faith.

"What I've learned is that God gives us the strength we need when we reach our place of need, not days or weeks or even moments before, when we're sitting around and fretting about the future possibilities."

Melinda and I ended our lunch, but as I drove home, I thought about the fears I was currently facing: the recurring illness of a family member; the consequences of choices being made by our almost-grown children; some deadlines at work that seemed impossible.

But I remembered what I had learned from Lois her long, last year: God doesn't promise that our journeys will be easy but does promise to walk alongside us and give us just enough light and just enough strength so that we can take one small step at a time. And when we come face-to-face with the thing we fear the most, he provides what we need.

And the fear disappears. Just like a mirage.

Footprint Scripture

Do not be afraid, for I am with you (Isa. 43:5).

Footprint Lessons

- When we trust God, he transforms our fears into faith.

- Fears are feelings we have about something that *might* happen in the future. We feel afraid when we imagine the possibilities without trusting how God will prepare us and provide for us.

- God walks alongside us and holds up just enough light to help us take one small step at a time.

- God gives us sufficient strength at our point of need, not weeks or months before, when we're fretting about possibilities.

- When we trust God, a fear about the future is like a mirage; it seems real until we get right up to it, and then it disappears.

Reflections

1. When you think about your future, what is your greatest fear?

2. Imagine your friend has exactly the same fear. What advice would you give her?

3. When you get up to the edge of that fear in your future, do you believe God will provide you with the strength you need? Why or why not? How does that change how you are dealing with your fears today?

4. In the past, have you experienced God's strength when you reached the edge of a fear? Explain.

5. If you are a parent, what are you teaching your children about facing their fears?

part four

Overcoming Temptations

God is faithful; he will not let you be tempted beyond what you can bear. But when you are tempted, he will also provide a way out so that you can stand up under it.

1 Corinthians 10:13

Along the pathway of life, temptations beckon and entice us. They seem so harmless, so subtle. In fact, they often look good.

Unknowingly, we take a wrong turn. We follow the wrong tracks and eventually find ourselves somewhere we don't want to be. Or shouldn't be.

So we turn around and get back on the right track again.

f o u r t e e n

Perfectionism

I have these pictures in my mind

"Do you consider yourself a perfectionist?" a friend asked as she watched me pluck a dandelion from my lawn. It was a hot summer afternoon, and we sat cross-legged on the grass while our children chased each other around the backyard like playful puppy dogs.

"Absolutely not!" I answered, without a moment's hesitation. "I can't think of a single area of my life in which I achieve perfection. I don't have a perfect house or perfect children. Obviously, I don't have a perfect lawn."

"I don't think it's achieving perfection so much as pursuing perfection," she said. "It's listening to the voices in our heads that say we *should* measure up to the pictures of perfection we carry around, especially as moms. Take labor and delivery, for instance. I had a picture in my mind of how I *should* deliver a baby. Painlessly. Quickly. Without medication. I made that picture out of the best parts of other people's descriptions. When my delivery didn't work out the way I pictured it, I felt like I'd fallen short of the standard."

"Me too," I confessed. "I assumed all good mothers used natural childbirth. But after spending several hours in hard labor, I gave up and begged, 'Bring on the painkillers. Knock me out. Wake me up next week.' Afterwards, I felt badly because I hadn't had a drug-free delivery."

Our conversation abruptly ended there. One child fell down, accused the other of pushing, and we were distracted by refereeing. But over the next few days, I became more aware of the pictures of perfection and the *I should* voices I carried around in my head.

Later that afternoon, for instance, I was folding laundry. My husband's cotton T-shirts were badly wrinkled because I hadn't responded when the dryer buzzer went off. In fact, that had been at least twenty-four hours earlier. (*Bad!* scolded the little *I should* voice in my head.) Then an image flashed through my mind of a woman I know who irons her husband's T-shirts . . . and the bed sheets . . . and the pillowcases . . . and the towels for her entire family. I tried to dismiss this preposterous picture, but as I stuffed the folded, wrinkled shirts into the drawer, I imagined the perfectly smooth shirts in the drawers at the other woman's house.

A couple days later, a friend called to say she was organizing a schedule of dinners to be taken to a new mom in the neighborhood. Would I like to sign up for an evening? Suddenly an image flashed into my mind of how this responsibility *should* be carried out: *Devise a menu, not too spicy, not too high in fat; just right for the new mom and hungry dad. Include the four basic food groups. Keep it fresh, but make it something they can freeze, in case they have too many leftovers. Use disposable containers so they don't have the hassle of returning them.*

I should be able to do this, the voice told me, but the idea of putting together such a portable meal made me panic. I have trouble getting all the parts of a dinner together at the same time in my own home! Still I said, "Sure, I'll do Thursday"—only because Thursday was farthest away. When Thursday rolled around, I ended up taking carry-out chicken and then feeling guilty because I hadn't created a homemade meal. Once again, I had fallen short of the perfect picture I had in my mind.

That summer, I became aware of the pictures of perfection I carried around in my mind, but they were minor compared to the picture I tried to live up to during an experience a few years later. It was after the birth of our last child, when I faced the first major surgery of my life—a hysterectomy. I dreaded the whole idea but decided I would get through this necessity easily and quickly.

"What's the shortest amount of time a person has stayed in the hospital with this kind of surgery?" I asked my doctor a few days before surgery.

He hesitated before answering.

"With your type of surgery, one lady stayed forty-eight hours, but she had some complications and came back." He emphasized the last part, because he must have suspected I was building an impossible-to-achieve picture of perfection in my mind.

Sure enough, I started calculating. I was basically healthy. Exercised regularly. And I came from sturdy stock. I'd check in on Monday morning and be home by Wednesday morning. Maybe sooner. Maybe I'd even set a new record. I liked physical challenges.

I went in on Monday as scheduled. My husband tells me I emerged from surgery late Monday afternoon, but I don't remember much until Tuesday morning—when I woke up and thought they forgot to sew me shut. Everything hurt. To breathe. To cough. To try to sit up. Timidly, I reached beneath my bandages. The long incision was sutured with steel staples!

A nurse came into the room.

"Well, good morning," she said much too cheerfully as she snapped open the blinds, filling the room with bright sunshine. "You seemed to have a restful night. And this morning, we're going to get up and get walking."

What did she mean by this *we* stuff? Surely I would never walk again. Surely I would stay in this bed forever. In a dark room. In silence.

My doctor came in and smiled knowingly when I told him I didn't feel so well.

Later that day, I did get up. The nurse made me do it. And then I walked across the room to a chair that seemed about four miles away. I sat down for a few moments and then crawled back into bed.

The stark truth was beginning to sink in. I was not some tough Super Lady that was going to make a miraculous recovery. I was a wimp, falling way short of the high expectations I set for myself. There was no way I was going to be home by Wednesday morning.

That night I couldn't sleep. I lay flat on my back in that hospital room looking up at the ceiling as the minutes ticked by slowly. But I had the feeling that was exactly where God wanted me—totally helpless and looking up at him—because he needed to get my attention about this pursuit of perfection.

It's as if he was telling me: *My child, too often you fill the screen of your mind with unrealistic expectations you set for yourself. Those are not my expectations for you. I don't expect you to be perfect or to perform like some Super Woman. I expect you to accept who you are and where you are. No one is perfect, and when you recognize that, you recognize your need for me.*

So why not wipe the screen clean of all your unrealistic pictures and clear out all those "I should" voices that aren't mine? Leave the expectations up to me. Let me fill in the blank screen with the picture of expectations I have for you.

Little did I know, as I lay in the darkness, still in pain, that I was on the road to recovery. In more ways than one.

Years later, I look back on that night with a vivid memory of the message I received.

Up to that point, I'd fallen into a pattern of pursuing perfectionism, a subtle temptation, because it often seemed I was merely setting good goals for myself. But most of them were impossible goals.

Also, I didn't see myself as a perfectionist because I didn't *achieve* perfection. But perfectionists are people who *pursue* perfection by creating those unrealistic pictures and expecting themselves to live up to them. And when they don't, they are disappointed with themselves and their circumstances. The *pursuit* of perfectionism robs people of the peaceful acceptance of themselves.

I have to keep reminding myself of that simple truth, because the subtle temptation of perfectionism constantly beckons me. For continual help, I turn to the Bible, which reminds me what God says about perfection.

God calls us to "be perfect . . . as your heavenly father is perfect" (Matt. 5:48), but when we examine the meaning of that word "perfect," we find that it means to be complete, mature, and holy. The definition has three parts:

First, to be *complete* means to be who I am and to accept who I am. It means to seek to achieve the goals for which I was created, not the goals for which someone else is created. I shouldn't set pictures in my mind that are based on someone else's experiences; I shouldn't compare myself to someone else. I must accept who I am, because God accepts who I am.

Second, to be *mature* means to be where I am, at my own level of growth and maturity, within my unique set of circumstances. Just as we don't expect our children to respond to life like adults, I shouldn't expect myself to respond to my challenges like someone who is older, wiser, or more experienced. Also, I need to observe and accept the circumstances around me at this moment in time.

Third, to be *holy* means to know I am in the process of growing and changing. I can pursue goodness and excellence and walk in the direction of perfection, but true perfection—to be without flaws—is not attainable in this lifetime, only in heaven. In the meantime, I need to accept the fact that I'm not perfect; I'm in process. I'm not flawless; I'm forgiven.

I'm still tempted by the pursuit of perfection and challenged to apply what I know about it. For example, in a few days, Lynn and I will be hosting a brunch at the apartment of our son, Derek, for some people who serve on the Young Life staff with him in Colorado Springs. Already I find myself building some expectations about the way we *should* host this gathering.

Though this is an extremely busy time and we are planning this long distance, I am thinking about the recipes I *should* try or food I *should* prepare ahead and freeze or the special table settings I *should* create. I've also started picturing how a particular friend of mine would handle this challenge. She used to be a caterer and loves entertaining. She thrives on this kind of challenge. It is her thing, but it is not mine.

As I feel this picture building in my mind, I recognize once again that I am being tempted by the pursuit of perfectionism, so I stop and ask myself, *What is wrong with this picture? Who is setting my standards?* Then I wipe the screen clear of my own expectations and seek God's picture of perfection for me.

First, in my calling to be complete, I need to be and accept who I am. I am not a great cook; I am an adequate cook. I don't often experiment with new recipes, so I shouldn't start this week. I don't need to impress someone with talents I don't have.

Second, in my calling to be mature, I need to acknowledge where I am. I need to look at my circumstances. I am carrying some extra responsibilities right now and I have less time than usual. This gathering is not in our home, so I should plan something simple that puts the priority on spending time with people, not on finding spatulas, wire whisks, and other necessary utensils. Then I need to be mature enough to accept my limitations.

And finally, in my calling to be holy, I need to recognize that I am not perfect, but I am in process. That gives me the freedom to plan a simple meal with some carry-out food and paper plates and know with confidence that my offering and honest efforts will please God—and that he will make it perfect for that time and place.

Am I a perfectionist? The open-hearted, truthful answer is yes, I am tempted by the pursuit of perfectionism. But I'm counting on an even greater truth . . . and that is God's promise to show me a way out of this temptation.

Footprint Scripture

. . . he who began a good work in you will carry it on to completion until the day of Christ Jesus (Phil. 1:6).

Footprint Lessons

- A perfectionist is not one who *achieves* perfection, but one who *pursues* perfection by setting unrealistic goals and then feeling dissatisfied when those goals are not met.

- The pursuit of perfectionism robs us of the peaceful acceptance of ourselves.

- When we recognize we are not perfect, we recognize our need for God.

- We are not perfect; we are in process.

- We are not flawless; we are forgiven.

Reflections

1. What is your definition of a perfectionist?

2. Are you a perfectionist? Why or why not?

3. Can you think of a time when you expected perfection of yourself? How might you handle that situation differently?

4. Who sets your standards? You? Your spouse? Your mother? A friend? God? How do those standards from different people differ?

5. Look at the Footprint Scripture (Phil. 1:6). How can you apply this verse to your own life?

f i f t e e n

Busyness

Busy is best . . . right?

"Down, Mommy!" eighteen-month-old Kendall demanded as she toddled after me through the family room, dragging a big picture book of Mother Goose rhymes. She first squatted down and then toppled backwards, sitting down on the carpet with a thud. She opened the book and pounded the floor beside her.

"Down, Mommy!" she repeated loudly and held out the book to me as I walked right by her.

"Maybe in a few minutes, sweetie," I half-promised, distracted by the paper in my hand that listed the phone numbers of some mothers in the preschool carpool. I needed to arrange a trade, because Lynn and I were going to an out-of-town convention for a few days. I also had to call the baby-sitter, write out a list of instructions for her, finish a writing project, and do the minutes for a YMCA board meeting that night.

The day seemed packed full.

So were most days. As the mother of three children, carrying on a part-time job at home, pursuing a respectable tennis game, and involved in a few community activities, I lived a hectic lifestyle. But I have to admit, the pace actually energized me. I liked

being busy. I liked the notations that filled the squares on my calendar. They gave my days a sense of purpose and gave me a feeling of accomplishment.

Just that morning after a tennis lesson, another mother had
watched me quickly gather up children, blankets, toys, and diapers
to race off to an appointment.

"I don't know how you get everything done," she said.

I assumed she meant that as a compliment.

"Hello, Mary?" I said . . .

"Down, Mommy!" Kendall commanded once more as she toddled over to me, sat down by my feet, and pounded the floor again.

"Shhh," I motioned, as I dialed the first number on my list.

The next afternoon, I sat on a grassy slope by a small lake near
the hotel where Lynn was attending the convention meetings. The
autumn air felt cool on my face and the sun warmed my back as I
watched little ripples blow gently across the surface of the water.

Our three children were home with the baby-sitter, more than
one hundred miles away. So here I sat, totally alone in this tran-
quil, idyllic setting, without any deadlines or phones or responsibilities for the first time in months.

I checked my watch. 2 P.M. The kids would be getting up from
their naps. I pictured them with their sleepy eyes and tousled hair.
I loved their cuddly waking up time, when, like limp rag dolls, they
snuggled into my arms. Suddenly I longed to be there for that
moment, to stretch it out and savor it in a way I almost never did.
Usually something else seemed more pressing.

I pictured Kendall waking up and marching right over to her
bookshelf and pulling out her favorite Mother Goose book and then
ordering the baby-sitter around.

"Down, Megan!" she probably commanded, hoping she had a
better chance with this new person than her own busy mother.

I hoped Megan would sit down and read to Kendall.

"Don't worry about the house or laundry," I had told her. "Just
spend time with the kids."

Why didn't I do what I told the baby-sitter to do?

I could think of only one answer—I was too busy.

I thought of my calendar by the phone at home, the squares filled with smudgy notations about committee meetings, deadlines, places to be. Had I allowed a full calendar to become a measurement of my significance? What about the important activities that weren't written down, like reading to Kendall? Were they overlooked because they weren't on the calendar?

I pictured Kendall following me around with her book the day before.

"Down, Mommy!" It was more of a plea than a command.

But at that moment I saw it as a "little need" and paid little attention.

In the solitude and stillness by the lake, I saw the importance of that moment and that "little need" very differently.

I longed for the opportunity to respond differently.

When my family asked me how I wanted to spend my birthday recently, I knew just the right answer. I wanted a few hours of solitude and stillness. Life had gotten too busy and I needed to sort through the chaos and think about priorities.

That's a solution I learned on the shore of that little lake years earlier, when I realized how stillness helps the sorting process. On that memorable afternoon, away from the distractions at home, I clearly saw the difference between the urgent and the important. The lesson was wrapped up in the powerful image of a toddler pounding the floor at my feet and pleading "Down, Mommy!" I had been too busy to recognize the importance of that message for me.

Since that day, I've started seeking solitude and stillness regularly so that my busyness doesn't numb me from knowing what's important. But through the years, I've learned that a mom has to be intentional about planning these times of stillness or they don't happen. It means trading kids with someone else or marking out a whole Saturday afternoon on the calendar weeks in advance. Or taking advantage of a birthday when we get to make requests about how we want to spend the day.

My places of solitude and stillness have varied, depending on how much time I have and how well I have planned. Sometimes I merely go on a long walk around our neighborhood or down into the fields below our house, where I can shut out the noise of people and traffic, and hear the birds and wind in the trees. Sometimes I get up early and watch the sun rise. Or I sit in a church chapel or on a park bench. Or I get in the car and drive somewhere, like up into the mountains near our home.

On my recent birthday, when I had the luxury of choosing my agenda for a whole day, I tried something different. I went to a Benedictine abbey just down the road from us. It's a retreat center where people can get a room or wander around the grounds for a time of solitude to listen to God.

On that day, I took my Bible, some water, an apple, paper, and a pen. I started off by reading about Mary and Martha, a couple of famous sisters in the Bible who had different responses to busyness (Luke 10:38–41). Martha reminds me of myself. As the story goes, Jesus came to their house for a visit one afternoon. Mary, the quieter, more contemplative sister, sat at his feet and listened to what he had to say. She had no trouble recognizing that this precious moment would not come around again, and that she needed to take advantage of the opportunity to hear Jesus teach.

"Make the most of life's irretrievable moments" is a motto that sums up Mary's response to life.

Martha, on the other hand, was distracted by the preparations for the evening meal, so she busied herself in the kitchen, intent on putting together a sumptuous feast for Jesus. I identify with her sense of responsibility.

"Down, Martha!" I could imagine Jesus saying, as he patted the floor next to his feet. But Martha went right on chopping and cooking and cleaning and fretting about her many urgent tasks, convinced of their importance. The tyranny of the urgent caused Martha to lose sight of the important.

In the hours of solitude and stillness at the abbey, I considered the ways I do things the same way as Martha. Often, I am distracted by the many pressing tasks at hand while missing something more important that is happening at my feet . . . perhaps a moment that will not come around again, like a child's desire to talk late at night, or a teenager's spontaneous invitation to go to a movie, or my husband's request that I ride along to do an errand.

I thought about my misconception that I should finish all the tasks on my "to do" list before allowing myself the privilege of taking time to invest in relationships. The truth is, I will never finish all the tasks on my "to do" list. In fact, I am certain I will die with an unfinished "to do" list. So I need to stop trying to get everything done, and start taking advantage of the opportunities to invest in others.

In sorting through my priorities during that time of solitude and stillness, I asked myself these questions:

Who or what is determining my agenda? Who am I seeking to please? What will matter most in five years?

If I knew I had one week left to live, how would I spend my time? If I gave my calendar to God, what would he change?

As I drove away from the abbey at the end of that day, I thanked God for the power of his still, small voice, which I hear most clearly in quiet places.

After a time of numbing busyness, I hear his voice gently telling me, "Down, Carol. Down, my child."

And I get the message. Loud and clear.

Footprint Scripture

But seek first his kingdom and his righteousness, and all these things will be given to you as well (Matt. 6:33).

Footprint Lessons

- Busyness numbs us and distracts us from recognizing what really matters.

- The tyranny of the urgent often causes us to lose sight of the important.

- A time of solitude and stillness helps us sort through the chaos and bring perspective to our priorities.

- A time of solitude and stillness helps us hear the still, small voice of God.

- Make the most of life's irretrievable moments.

Reflections

1. In what ways is your life too busy?

2. How does the tyranny of the urgent distract you and cause you to lose sight of what's important? How do you define the difference between busyness and importance?

3. What does it mean to you to "make the most of life's irretrievable moments"?

4. Read the story about Mary and Martha in Luke 10:38–41. Are you more like Mary or Martha? Explain.

5. How might you benefit from a time of solitude and stillness? When and how could you plan such a time in the next month? Where and how would you spend it? What questions would you ask yourself in that time of stillness?

sixteen

Success

Who needs another plastic trophy?

When our three children were little, I got bitten by the tennis bug. Bad.

In the beginning, I liked everything about the game. The fresh air and exercise. The *thunk* of the ball solidly hitting the sweet spot on the racket. The ability to see improvement with practice. And those little plastic fake gold trophies that signified success.

One day shortly after I started playing, I stopped to get a drink of water at another tennis player's house following a game on her neighborhood court. She had a whole shelf-full of those little plastic trophies.

"Wow," I said, as I admired her display. "You must be really good."

Eventually, our family joined a small local tennis club that offered lessons, a team, and a ladder of rankings prominently displayed on the wall inside the front door. As you got better and won games, your name moved up that ladder of success for all to see.

This tennis club also offered baby-sitting, which not only made my tennis possible, but—I rationalized—also made my tennis good for the kids, because they could play with friends. And it gave some structure to our long summer days. A win-win situation, I concluded.

My kids didn't always see it that way.

"Mom, do we have to go to the tennis club again today?" five-year-old Derek asked as I woke him up early one warm summer morning.

"Yes, but you'll see your friends there and we'll pack a bunch of snacks and you'll have fun," I assured him as I hurriedly helped him dress. "You'll need to eat breakfast in the car," I said. "We're running late."

With that, I hastily herded five-year-old Derek, four-year-old Lindsay, and one-year-old Kendall out the door, along with all our paraphernalia for a marathon morning courtside. Sometimes I would take a lesson, other times I would play a ladder match, and sometimes I just took out a bucket of balls and practiced serving. At least in this area of my life, I could see that my investment of time brought tangible success. How many serves out of ten will go in this time? Only six? Let me try again. Whew, seven this time. Better. I'll try again. My progress whetted my appetite, so that I practiced even more.

I even organized some Sundays around my tennis obligations. I often scheduled a ladder match after church, because Lynn was content to be home with the kids. One particular Sunday, church ran a little long. The kids dawdled in their Sunday school rooms, and people stopped to talk to us. I kept checking my watch and getting nervous. I didn't like having church interfere with my tennis match. I'd have to forfeit if I ran much later. *Could I still make it?* I thought, agitated.

I did finally make it to my tennis match that day, a little late and a little flustered. And I lost. That meant I'd have to practice more and try harder next time.

Eventually, I started playing in a few local tournaments, and I'll never forget the day I brought home my first small fake gold trophy.

"Wow, Mom, you must be good," Derek said admiringly.

I puffed right up at the recognition. Maybe I could get better. Maybe with a few more lessons, I could improve my second serve and move up the ladder.

The next summer, I tried even harder. But it seemed the more I played, the less satisfied I felt with the way I played. This growing frustration began to take away some of the fun, but not much of the drive. I wanted to get better.

That summer, I aimed especially for the all-club, end-of-the-year tournament over Labor Day weekend. I asked for my family's support so that I could practice every day those last two weeks. "If this is important to you, I'll support you," Lynn told me, and planned his evenings so he could be home with the kids while I practiced pounding the ball against the backboard at the courts.

I entered all three categories in the tournament—singles, women's doubles with my friend Lois, and mixed doubles with one of the best players at the club.

Amazingly, and thanks to some great doubles partners, I won all three categories.

"A clean sweep. This is a first for our club," the man said when he handed out the trophies. "Congratulations. You must be proud of your success."

For some reason, I felt a little let down as I carried home my three plastic trophies. When I walked in the front door, I set them down on the kitchen counter and stood back to look at them.

And wondered. . . . *So what?*

What is so important about three plastic trophies?

And if I keep playing like this, what will I have gained in three years? A better backhand and a few more plastic trophies?

So what?

"So, why don't you play tennis anymore?"

I still get that question sometimes, though it's been nearly fifteen years since I played much tennis. I actually have several answers:

"I don't have as much time."

"I suffered a ruptured disc years ago, and I can't play like I used to."

"I'm not very good anymore."

All those answers are true, but they aren't the *real* truth.

The real truth is, I don't play tennis anymore because on the day I brought those three plastic trophies home, something happened inside me. I now see that "something" was a loving nudge from God that helped me realize tennis was ruling my life. And if I kept going like I was going, a growing collection of plastic trophies would sum up the meaning of success in my life.

Is that what I wanted—to reach the end of my life with a case full of plastic trophies?

Clearly the answer was no.

So I stopped playing tennis. Almost cold turkey. It's not that tennis is bad. But it wasn't good for me at that time. With its ladders and rankings and other tempting, tangible markers of success, it pushed the wrong buttons in me and lured me into giving it greater importance in my life than it deserved.

Sometimes when I recognize my vulnerability to certain temptations like tennis, I have to avoid them altogether. Besides, with tennis, I couldn't step back and simply play the game at a lower level, because I'm not good enough to play decently without lots of practice. And I don't enjoy playing poorly and losing. So I pretty much stopped playing.

I can come up with lots of reasons for why the sport gripped me. For one thing, I never had the opportunity to play competitive sports in high school. The whole experience tasted new and exciting. But more important, I lived in a world without many tangible measurements of success or much recognition of achievement or even affirmation. Young children don't rave about the superiority of homemade play dough over the store-bought kind. No one gives out certificates of achievement (suitable for framing) for successfully potty training a toddler or recognizes a mother for the patience and perseverance she displayed in that process. The mother of young children doesn't get many tangible trophies marking success for her investment of time.

Because of my tennis days, however, I learned something about the difference between tangible and intangible trophies of success, and the importance of each.

Tangible trophies—like my plastic fake gold tennis trophies— don't have lasting value and don't bring lasting satisfaction like intangible trophies do. In fact, the more I pursued the success represented by those tennis trophies, the less they satisfied. More plastic trophies brought less satisfaction.

The same is true with tangible trophies of success in other areas of life. In business, the trophies are titles or power or money. But a little bit of money hardly ever satisfies.

The truth is, we can't get enough of the kind of success that doesn't really satisfy. We always want more. We always have an emptiness that those tangible trophies can't fill. I'm now convinced that God plants that truth in our hearts to nudge us and show us the way out of our temptations. As we recognize his nudge and turn away from the temptations that don't satisfy, we discover the areas of success that do bring lasting satisfaction.

What is success that satisfies?

Through the years, I am learning that the success that satisfies comes from investing myself in what God values. Success that satisfies is found in relationships: a love for him and a love for other people.

What is the trophy or reward for success in these areas? It is intangible.

It is the joy that comes after the "I'm sorry" that mends a rift in a relationship. It is the peace that comes after yielding my need to be right in a silly disagreement with my husband. It is the love I feel for others after spending time praying and praising God for his goodness.

On a shelf in my clothes closet, I still display my three plastic tennis trophies I won in that club tournament. Year by year they gather more dust, but I keep them there in a private but prominent place so I can see them every day and remember the meaning of success and the kind of trophies that matter most.

Footprint Scripture

So we fix our eyes not on what is seen, but on what is unseen. For what is seen is temporary, but what is unseen is eternal (2 Cor. 4:18).

Footprint Lessons

- You can't get enough of success that doesn't really satisfy. God puts that truth in our hearts to nudge us and give us a way out when we face temptations such as money, power, possessions, or the accumulation of trophies.

- Success in God's eyes is not measured by what we accomplish or what we do, but by what we surrender of ourselves to him.

- Tangible trophies don't bring a satisfying or meaningful measurement of success in life. At the end of our lives, someone will trash our trophies.

- Intangible trophies are the rewards we receive from investing in what matters to God: a loving relationship with him and others.

Reflections

1. What is your definition of success?

2. What kinds of trophies are rewarded for that success? Are they tangible or intangible?

3. How has your definition of success changed through the years?

4. If you were awarded a trophy for your success today, what would this trophy represent?

5. If you were awarded a trophy at the end of your life, what would you hope that trophy represented?

6. How are you working toward that trophy today?

seventeen

Beauty

Perfect fingernails make me feel pretty

I sat on the floor in a circle at Kendall's preschool with a group of mothers and children singing, "Where is Thumbkin? Where is Pointer? Where is Middle-Man?"

Every new phrase brought a new set of fingers from behind our backs.

We were having great, giggly fun . . . except for one thing. I was feeling especially frumpy that day, and next to me sat a pretty mother. With perfect fingernails.

As the song went on, I felt the lure.

I too wanted perfect fingernails. Surely they would make me just as pretty.

This wasn't the first time I longed for perfect fingernails. At meetings, I watched women make dramatic hand gestures with perfect fingernails. At the grocery store, I watched women check ingredients on labels with perfect fingernails. At the bank, I watched the tellers punch buttons on the computer with perfect fingernails. In my mind, perfect fingernails made these women pretty.

As I sat at Kendall's preschool that day, I studied my stubby, uneven, fat fingernails. On the way home, I stopped at the grocery store and nonchalantly dropped a fingernail kit into my cart. The box promised I could create "pretty, perfect fingernails, instantly and easily, in the privacy of your own home."

They were definitely wrong on the instant and easy part.

As soon as I got home, I disappeared into the bedroom, closed the door, and spent the next two hours shaping, glueing, filing, polishing, and refiling my ten new nails. Finally I emerged with an at-home, non-professional-looking attempt at perfect fingernails.

But for me, they were a vast improvement.

For several days, I couldn't take my eyes off my fingernails. I began talking with my hands more and pointing a lot, at something in the newspaper or a phone number in a list. I touched my face more often, resting my chin in my hands. My kids said I was "acting hot" with my new nails, which wasn't meant as a compliment, but I brushed their words aside.

I felt kind of pretty.

Yet something strange started happening. I found myself worrying about my perfect fingernails and protecting them. I couldn't do lots of regular things, like make beds with fitted sheets, or pull weeds, or help my daughters saddle their horses. I started carrying glue and Band-Aids around in my purse for small on-the-spot repairs or cover ups, and constantly fiddled with my broken or ragged nails—especially early in the morning, a time usually set aside for praying or reading my Bible. It always seemed like that's when I noticed new flaws in my nails. So instead of praying, I often ended up filing or repairing my nails.

Sometimes I got upset with other people when something happened to my nails.

Like the afternoon our family attended a big picnic party and I pulled a tab off a pop can for my daughter Lindsay without realizing what it would do to my perfect "Middle-Man" nail.

I snapped the tab—and half of my fingernail—right off.

"Rats!" I said angrily, handing Lindsay the can, as if my broken nail was her fault.

"Mom, those fingernails make you mean," Lindsay told me, and then marched off.

For the rest of the afternoon I felt self-conscious and irritated. Irritated with my nails and irritated with myself. And my feelings began spilling over into the world around me.

By the time I got home, I knew that my fingernails had to go.

They made me feel pretty, but Lindsay was right. They also made me mean.

So I disappeared into our bedroom and pulled them off, one-by-one, all nine-and-a-half of them. When I emerged, my nails looked extra ragged, but I actually felt liberated.

I knew I'd been in bondage to those perfect fingernails. I had thought they would make me feel pretty, but the pursuit of them was taking me in the wrong direction. I recognized the signals and so did others around me. It was those out-of-control feelings that helped me know it was time to get back on track.

Many years have passed since my episode with perfect finger-nails, but I've often found myself in similar situations, lured by something I think will make me feel pretty, such as a new jacket or shoes or a new exercise plan. The pattern is usually the same. If I start pursuing the temptation with a zeal that gives it more importance than it deserves, I get that same uncomfortable, out-of-control feeling I experienced with the perfect fingernails. It's always a sure signal that I'm heading in the wrong direction.

Since my bout with the perfect fingernails, I've learned a simple response that helps me sort through such temptations. It comes from a familiar reminder I used to give our children when I wanted them to beware of possible dangers or temptations lurking in their paths. It is the old *Stop! Look!* And *Listen!* commands, and it almost always gets me back on track and heading in the right direction.

Here's how it worked for me recently when I was tempted to buy some new clothes I thought would make me feel pretty.

It was the word "sale" that lured me into the woman's clothing store that day.

"May I help you?" the eager saleslady asked as I headed toward the sale rack.

"I'm just looking, really." I tried to sound nonchalant. The truth was, I'd been feeling particularly frumpy lately. I'd gone back to work in an office and realized I needed to update my wardrobe. But small specialty stores like this one usually made me feel self-conscious. I didn't like trying on clothes in front of overly attentive salesladies.

"Anything in particular you need?" she asked, appearing again at my elbow.

"I have a new job . . ." I stammered in a moment of vulnerability, and then wondered why I'd told her that.

Before I knew it, I was in a dressing room and she was bringing me clothes.

"That's a wonderful color on you," she gushed as I pulled on a coral print dress. "Turn around. . . . hmmm . . . yes," she evaluated. "That style is flattering. Here, try on this suit and let me bring you a scarf."

With that, she disappeared and soon returned with three scarves, a belt, jacket, and two skirts.

"These are such smart mix-and-match combinations. Certainly a wise investment," she said as she twisted an ordinary scarf into a fashionable bow at my neck. "This is *the look* these days."

I've never worn scarves because I can't tie them and I always feel like I'm trying to be someone I am not. But as I looked in the mirror at the colorful scarf-bow, I felt tempted. Maybe I could pull off this look. Maybe this would create a "new me." Maybe I could be just like all those sophisticated women who command attention because they appear so sure of themselves.

Soon the dressing room was filled with "wise investments" guaranteed to transform me into someone I wanted to be. Fashionable. Self-assured. Professional. I glanced at the pile on the chair and something gripped me.

I wanted them all.

I needed them all.

I was certain they would make me feel pretty.

They were a wise investment.

Then I stopped and took a deep breath. I recognized that familiar out-of-control feeling.

I was headed in the wrong direction.

"I need time to think," I told the saleslady. "Would you please put these things on hold for me?" I handed her the pile, marched out of the store, and took another deep breath.

Stop! As soon as I recognized the lure of this temptation and my out-of-control feelings, I knew I needed to stop. I needed to separate myself from an immediate decision and from the temptation. I needed to find some time and space to sort through my responses.

Look! I needed to look at this temptation. Was it harmful or wrong? In this case, the answer was no. In fact, nice clothes or colorful silk scarves or perfect fingernails are not wrong in themselves. The desire to look nice reflects our understanding that we are people of value, that we are worth the effort of taking good care of ourselves. Those things become wrong only when we pursue them with an out-of-control zeal that gives them more importance than they deserve. Or when we start believing that they will transform us into different or better people. Or when our pursuit of these things distracts us from pursuing God or causes us to act contrary to his will or lose sight of his truth.

Listen! What was God's perspective on this issue? I needed to listen to him. Sometimes that means going to the Bible or seeking advice from a trusted Christian friend. In this case, I knew God's promise about what he values when it comes to beauty and appearance. Though most people judge us by our external appearance, God looks on the heart, or what's on the inside. He doesn't value or love a person more for having perfect fingernails or nice clothes or colorful scarves. He is satisfied with us and our appearance in old clothes or new clothes. God loves us for who we are and who we are becoming. When we accept this truth and put the temptation into God's perspective, we experience a freedom to have perfect fingernails or nice clothes, because those things won't distract us from God's truth.

How did *Stop! Look!* And *Listen!* work in helping me sort through my temptations in the midst of my shopping spree? After giving myself twenty-four hours to think about those clothes, I went back to the store the next day.

"I knew you'd be back," the attentive saleslady said as she brought out the pile of clothing.

"I've decided to get these things," I said, picking out three items from the pile.

"Is that all?" she asked, a bit surprised.

I nodded.

She tallied my total and handed me the package with a smile.

"You made wise choices," she said. "Especially that scarf. It will transform your whole personality."

"Thanks." I said, and left.

Footprint Scripture

Man looks at the outward appearance, but the LORD *looks at the heart* (1 Sam.16:7).

Footprint Lessons

- Those things that make us feel pretty—nice clothes or perfect fingernails or exercise programs—are not wrong unless the pursuit of those things becomes more important than the pursuit of God.

- Put the pursuit of beauty into God's perspective.

- When we feel we're following a temptation in the wrong direction, we should *Stop! Look!* And *Listen! Stop* and buy yourself some time; *look* at the temptation and ask if it is wrong or harmful; and *listen* to what God says about this issue.

- Our source of value and self-worth is not found in our appearance, but in our hearts.

Reflections

1. What makes you feel pretty?

2. When have you felt tugged by an out-of-control pursuit of something that makes you feel pretty?

3. What is the importance of beauty in the world today? What is considered beautiful? How do you agree or disagree with the cultural answers to the quest for beauty?

4. Who do you admire for her beauty and why?

5. How have your ideas about beauty changed through the years? Do you believe that having perfect fingernails or nice clothes is wrong? Explain.

6. We are told that "God looks on the heart." What does this mean to you?

part five

Finding the Way

Stand at the crossroads and look . . .
ask where the good way is, and walk in it,
and you will find rest for your souls.

Jeremiah 6:16

Life is exhilarating, confusing, and often unpredictable. It is filled with choices and questions:

Who am I?

What is the meaning and purpose of my life?

What is truth, and where can I find it?

Sometimes we long for a road map to show us the way; a reliable set of guidelines to keep us on track. To give us directions about where to go and how to get there. To find the best route—and which ones to avoid.

And then we are told something we don't fully understand . . .

God is the Way.

eighteen

The Road Map
Is a Relationship

How do I begin?

"When did you become a Christian?"

The question sounded a bit odd to me, asked by another young mother as we sat next to each other in a circle of metal folding chairs on the first day of a Bible study. I had felt a bit apprehensive about joining this Bible study. Surely everyone here knew more about the Bible than I did. But I heard they offered a good children's program, and when you're a mom with young kids, you do lots of things because they might be good for your children.

When did I become a Christian?

Wasn't that like asking me when I became a good person, or when I learned the difference between right and wrong? I didn't know a moment *when*. Did that mean I was missing something?

I assumed I'd always been a Christian. After all, when I was a child, we always put up a crèche with baby Jesus at Christmastime. Sometimes we went to church, especially to the sunrise services in a local park each Easter. And sometimes we said grace before meals, like at Thanksgiving. I also learned the Lord's Prayer as a child.

So I assumed I was a Christian.

When I was about thirteen, I was baptized in a mountain meadow with my sister and two younger brothers. My parents thought everyone should get baptized, and they felt closest to God in the mountains. We didn't know the pastor; it was someone my mother found who said he'd be happy to baptize us on a Sunday afternoon in a meadow. Though I didn't really understand what baptism meant, I assumed that made me a Christian, right?

When I got to high school, I sometimes went to church by myself, drawn by a longing I couldn't explain. After I met Lynn in college, we often went to church together, and we got married in the same church that we had been attending pretty regularly now. In fact, we were members of that church. So that meant I was a Christian, right?

I knew that God is love, and he loves me . . . and here I was at this Bible study, so didn't that make me a Christian? So what did this question mean . . . *When* did I become a Christian?

What was the right answer?

All these thoughts zoomed through my head as I paused, seeking the correct answer.

Just then the Bible study leader interrupted my thoughts.

"Let's open with a prayer," she said, bowing her head.

"Lord Jesus," she prayed, *"May we open our eyes to your presence in our lives and may each person here come to know you in a personal way through this Bible study."*

I felt really confused.

"When did you become a Christian . . . and what does 'becoming a Christian' mean?"

This honest question came from a young woman who stopped by our house recently to drop off a book she had borrowed.

Her eyes filled with tears as she asked me about finding faith. She had attended church off and on since childhood, but felt confused by some troubling situations in her life. She was on the verge of ending a relationship with a serious boyfriend and was caught up with the responsibilities of a demanding new career that made her question the cost of success and her ability to measure up to company standards. She felt surprised by an emptiness she thought her career was going to fill.

I gave her a hug and then told her my own story about finding an answer to that question about becoming a Christian. It went back to the year I attended that Bible study.

When I joined the study that year, I assumed I was a Christian, but something was missing in my life. I was trying to be a good person, but I felt frustrated because I wasn't good enough or patient enough or loving enough or joyful enough. I felt inadequate and longed for a sense of affirmation and peace.

I now know that's how God works in our lives. He allows us to come face-to-face with our longings and inadequacies, and then he puts us in a particular place at a particular time where we begin to realize that our longing is really a longing for him. He creates a God-hunger in our hearts, and then he meets that need by revealing himself through a Bible study or another person or the words of a song or something we hear on a radio program.

I'd been aware of my God-hunger since high school, but in that Bible study, I finally realized something about God's plan I'd never understood before: God meets our needs and fills our longings through a personal relationship with his son Jesus. That's what it means to become a Christian.

I had been operating on some misconceptions. I used to think that becoming a Christian was something that happened automatically, like becoming a Smith because you were born into the Smith family. Or that you became a Christian from trying to be a good person or attending church. But we don't become Christians automatically. And Christianity isn't a bunch of rules or tedious efforts; it's a relationship with Jesus that begins by recognizing who Jesus is and recognizing our need for him.

The Bible says that Jesus is the Son of God, sent to be our Savior, and that we all are sinners in need of a Savior. Sinning means more than doing just the obviously wrong things, like lying or stealing or cheating on income tax returns. Sinning also means falling short of God's perfection, in the way we fail to show love to others, or get impatient, or want to have our own way, or put our own needs first. It means being imperfect, and these imperfections separate us from a perfect God.

But God doesn't want that separation. He created us to be in a loving relationship with him, and he desires that we live eternally with him in heaven. So he has provided a way to bring us back into a relationship with him. That "way" is our personal relationship with his Son, Jesus, who came not only as that baby in the manger at Christmas but also as our Savior, who willingly died on the cross so that his death would pay the penalty for our sins past, present, and future.

The important part is our choice of a personal response. Do we choose to believe that Jesus is who he says he is? Do we recognize our need for him?

If the answer is yes, we simply tell that to Jesus in a prayer that might go something like this: *"Jesus, I'm confused and tired of trying to be a good person, because I know I am not good enough. I am a sinner. And I know that you died on the cross to forgive my sins. I need your forgiveness. I want to know you as my Lord and Savior. I don't exactly know what all that means, Jesus, but I want you to come into my life and make me into the person you want me to be. Amen."*

With this prayer, Jesus holds out his hand. We take his hand, and he comes into our lives and walks alongside us and begins to transform us from the inside out.

For some people, becoming a Christian happens in a single, dramatic life-altering moment of saying this prayer. For others, like me, the moment of becoming a Christian has a fuzzier start. I had never said a prayer exactly like that, so I didn't have a single moment I could point to and say "That's the day *when* I became a Christian."

I heard an analogy once that describes this difference between these two experiences. For some people, becoming a Christian is like snapping on an electric light in a dark room. They hear the message about Jesus, pray a prayer of acceptance, and instantly the light transforms the darkness. For others, the light comes more slowly, like the gradual process of night turning into day. Even if you stayed awake all night, you couldn't be sure of the exact moment when night becomes day. Knowing the moment does not matter as much as recognizing with assurance that you are now walking in the daylight.

In my Bible study that year, I recognized that I had been walking in the light of some of this truth and had made partial personal responses. I already knew about Jesus, but I wasn't acting like I believed his promises. So one day when I came home from Bible study, I claimed this promise of assurance:

> . . . if you confess with your mouth, "Jesus is Lord," and believe in your heart that God raised him from the dead, you will be saved. For it is with your heart that you believe and are justified, and it is with your mouth that you confess and are saved (Rom. 10:9–10).

I marked the date in my Bible by that verse, and from that day forward, I could claim a moment when I knew with assurance I had a personal relationship with Jesus.

I learned so much in my Bible study that year. I learned that *when* I became a Christian didn't matter as much as *whether* I knew with assurance that I have a personal relationship with Jesus right now.

I learned that whenever I feel I'm not good enough, Jesus understands and accepts me. And those longings or fears or temptations help to remind me of my need for him, because he is always enough and always gives me enough. Enough strength. Enough love. Enough patience. I don't know how that happens, except that God promises to comfort us through a relationship with Jesus, who says "I am the way."

When I finished telling this story to my young friend, she said that was the first time she'd heard that description of what it means to become a Christian, and she wanted to think about it.

I understood. Most people have to hear that message several times before they respond; most—like me—respond slowly. But as she said good-bye and left that evening, I prayed that in her loneliness or emptiness or discouragement, she would see and follow in Jesus' footprints of faith. Because, he promises, "I am the way."

Footprint Scripture

I am the way and the truth and the life. No one comes to the Father except through me (John 14:6).

Footprint Lessons

- Christianity is a relationship.

- Becoming a Christian is not automatic; it is the result of a deliberate choice to enter into a personal relationship with Jesus. Christianity begins with a prayer, confessing our need for Christ.

- The basic truths of the Gospel message are:
  We are all sinners, and our sin separates us from God (Rom. 3:23; 6:23)
  God created us to be in relationship with him and has a solution to this problem of separation (John 3:16)
  The penalty for our sins was paid through the death of Jesus on the cross (John 14:6; Rom. 5:8)
  We enter into relationship with God through Jesus, as we receive him as our Lord and Savior and receive his forgiveness for our sins (John 1:12)

- Jesus said, "I am the way and the truth and the life" (John 14:6):
  "I am the way": Follow me. I am the pathway to knowing God.
  "I am the truth": I will guide you and show you how to make the right choices and this truth will free you from your burdens.
  "I am the life": I will sustain you and give you eternal life.

160

Reflections

1. Do you have an emptiness or longing in your life? How do you deal with these feelings? What helps you when you feel empty or lonely?

2. The Bible says we all have the problem of sin in our lives. How do you solve that problem in your life? Can you forgive yourself for your imperfections?

   Do you understand how Jesus can solve that problem for you? Explain.

3. If you are not a Christian, how do you imagine your life might change if you became a Christian?

4. Where are you in the process of seeking a personal relationship with Jesus?

5. Some people describe the process of becoming a Christian this way: "I gave what I knew of myself to what I knew of Jesus." What does this mean to you?

6. If you desire a personal relationship with Jesus, when would be a good time to start that relationship?

nineteen

Rules of the Road

The secret is training . . . not trying

I got up about 6 A.M., made some coffee, and then sat down at the kitchen counter, appreciating the stillness of the house and watching the soft glow of the sunrise appear on the eastern horizon. This was my favorite time of day. In the freshness of a new dawn, I liked to sit quietly and gather some strength. Especially for "The Launching Period," that hectic time when one husband and two elementary school-aged children scrambled to get up and out the door, while one preschooler tried to follow them.

Somehow I always felt responsible for shaping everybody's mood for the day.

So I liked this time to myself. Usually I would set some goals for the day and then tell God about them in a prayer-promise.

On this day, filled with early-morning optimism, I vowed this prayer-promise: *Today, Lord, I will be patient and kind and loving. I will help launch each member of the family into the day with a positive attitude. I will put their needs first as they try to get out the door. Today, I won't worry or lose my patience. I won't let their normal requests push my buttons. Amen.*

I was determined to make my efforts work.

Then I went to wake the children. One by one, they started wandering into the kitchen. They pushed their stools up to the kitchen counter and looked at me sleepily, as if waiting for a jump-start. From me.

"Good morning, my precious cherubs," I said cheerfully. "And what kind of cereal will it be today?" I asked, as I started into my Magic Mommy routine, quickly moving around the kitchen, making everything happen while they watched.

I unloaded the dishwasher, poured the juice, handed out the cereal bowls, toasted the bagels, and got out the lunch stuff.

I congratulated myself on the enthusiastic tone I was setting. But I have to admit, as I stood there across the counter from them, waiting for their orders, I felt a little like a short order cook in a fast food restaurant. Not a good feeling.

Meanwhile, the sleepy cereal eaters started slurping and sipping.

I began making some sandwiches.

Then they started in.

"Mom, I don't like lettuce anymore."

"Yuk! This orange juice tastes sick. Here, you try it, Mom!"

"Mom, where is that pink permission form I gave you last week in the car? I gotta' have it today!"

"Mom, I need a check for the Picture Lady because today is retakes."

"Mom, my permission slip!"

"Mom, can you cut this rubber band out of my hair?"

I patiently listened. I took out the lettuce. I tasted the juice. I got out my checkbook. (I had no clue where the permission slip was.) Then I opened the drawer to reach for the scissors. But the scissors were gone.

And something started to unravel inside me.

"Who took the scissors?" I demanded.

All three merely stared at me blankly.

"We have a real problem here," I said, trying to control my tone of voice as I rummaged through the drawer. "Somebody around here takes things and doesn't put them back." My voice was getting louder. "First it's the pencil by the phone, then the tweezers in the bathroom, and now it's the kitchen scissors. We can't operate this way!"

I slammed the drawer closed as if to punctuate my statement with an exclamation mark and turned to the line-up of cereal eaters, who were watching me, wide-eyed. We all knew that Mom had lost it. Again.

And it was only 7:48 in the morning.

My prayer-promise hadn't lasted long.

Why does this happen, God? I wondered in a silent prayer-question as I headed down the hall in search of a pair of scissors.

I try, but I can't seem to act like I know you want me to act. Or maybe I can for about fifteen minutes, but it doesn't last. I thought being a Christian meant this struggle would get easier. I don't get it, God.

As I sit here alone at the same kitchen counter this morning, some fifteen years later, I think back to those hectic days when the house erupted with the sights and sounds of young children, and I tried so hard to be patient but often lost it. And then felt frustrated.

I didn't get it.

I get it better now. The secret seems so simple, yet I made the struggle so hard.

It's because I was *trying* too hard. I thought my patience came from my self-effort or determination to be patient. But now I know that it does not come from trying; it comes from *training*—training in the habit of following after Jesus. Patience flows naturally from my relationship with him.

Though I knew this in my head, I didn't understand it until I was trying to run a race a few years ago. The race is called the Bolder Boulder, a six-mile annual community event that draws about thirty-five thousand runners. I've participated every year, but this particular year, I didn't have time to train. I assumed I'd get caught up in the spirit of the race and sheer effort and determination would carry me.

It did for the first couple of miles, but by the third mile, as I started up a small hill, I knew I was in trouble. My lungs burned and my legs ached. Even my most determined "I-think-I-can" attitude couldn't keep me going. I had to stop running and start walking.

If I had trained for this race, it would be easier, I told myself. *Trying hard isn't going to be enough. Trying isn't going to give me the strength or ability.*

Obviously, I didn't do well in the race that day, but as I walked the last several miles, I had plenty of time to think about the difference between trying and training. The analogy of the that race to my Christian "race" has helped me ever since.

I can try to be more patient, kind, and loving. But no matter how hard I try, my human effort and determination won't take me very far. The source of my own strength and ability is too limited and inconsistent.

Jesus explains this truth to his disciples by giving them a powerful word picture the night before his death. He tells them about abiding in the vine:

> I am the vine; you are the branches. If a man remains in me and I in him, he will bear much fruit; apart from me you can do nothing (John 15:5).

He tells the disciples—and therefore us too—that we can't live up to God's standards merely by trying hard or through our self-efforts. The ability and source of our strength will come only from our connection to the vine, from our relationship with Jesus.

Consider the branch of an apple tree. That branch does not produce apples by its own efforts. The branch alone has no ability to produce apples. It bears the fruit of the tree only because of its connection to the trunk, through which the life-giving water flows.

We are the same way. The traits we desire to experience and reflect are love, joy, peace, patience, and kindness. They are called the fruit of the Spirit and are the traits Jesus displayed in his life. But we don't produce those traits in ourselves by trying. We bear those fruits, those reflections of Jesus, as a result of abiding in the vine or being in relationship with him.

To abide means to be in an intimate relationship and to recognize our dependence upon that connection. It means to be certain that nothing hinders that relationship or gets in the way of our connection to that relationship.

If we want to be more loving or kind or patient, we don't focus on the self-effort of trying to be more loving; we train ourselves to focus on Jesus. We turn our eyes upon Jesus. We recognize our dependence upon him. We read the Bible and pray and listen to him. That is the essence of abiding.

As Thomas à Kempis says, "Christianity is nothing more than seeing Jesus face to face." Christianity means developing a friendship with Jesus, and out of that relationship flows the miracles of love and peace and patience in our lives.

I don't exactly know how that happens, but I got an idea when I took my playful four-month-old golden retriever Boaz to puppy obedience class at the local humane society.

"A puppy's obedience comes from his ability to focus on the master, regardless of the distractions or circumstances," the teacher told us as class started. "So you're going to train your puppy to keep his eyes on you by using the simple command 'Watch me!'"

For the next several days, I used doggie treats to train my roly-poly puppy to watch me. The most amazing thing happened. As he learned to lock eyes with me, he learned to sit and stay. Out of that training and our connected relationship flowed his ability to do what he was supposed to do.

His ability came from training, not trying.

It seems both a mystery and a miracle. The world is filled with self-help books and seminars and support groups to help us try to be more patient and kind and loving and good, but the Bible tells us we're looking for strength and ability in all the wrong places. We do not produce these results in our lives by trying or self-effort. It comes from training ourselves to keep our eyes on Jesus. From following hard after him. From understanding and experiencing his love for us. From abiding in the vine.

Even though I know this truth, I like to get up early in the morning and think about it at the start of each day. It's all part of my training plan.

Footprint Scripture

*Abide in me, and I in you. As the branch cannot
bear fruit by itself, unless it abides in the vine; neither can you, unless you abide in me . . . for apart
from me you can do nothing (John 15:4, 5 RSV).*

Footprint Lessons

- How can we be more loving, patient and kind? Not by
  trying. . . . but by training ourselves to follow after Jesus.

- Self-effort doesn't take us very far. We soon run out of
  steam.

- The world is filled with self-help books and seminars
  that tell us to reach inside ourselves and find the
  strength we need. But this source is too shallow and
  inconsistent. Our strength comes from our relationship
  with Jesus.

- We don't produce the traits of love and joy and peace
  in our lives. We bear those qualities because of our connection to Jesus.

Reflections

1. How do you understand the difference between *trying* and *training*?

2. Describe a character trait you are trying to change in yourself. How might training shift your viewpoint?

3. In John 15, Jesus gives his disciples a word picture about the vine and the branches and tells them to "Abide in me." What does that mean to you?

4. Jesus also tells the disciples, and therefore us, that "Apart from me you can do nothing." Do you believe this? Explain.

5. Christianity is a relationship. How do you intentionally deepen your relationship with Jesus?

Checking
the Rearview Mirror

The phone rang one morning recently.

It was my friend Dale. Even though we'd completed our commitment to a year-long mentoring program, we'd become friends and still talked regularly.

"What's up?" I asked, but then I heard the sound of a crying baby in the background, and I knew what was up. It was her baby, who was teething.

When I started writing this book, Dale was two weeks from the delivery of her first child, whom we called Simon during her pregnancy. But her delivery day finally arrived and—behold!—Simon became Savannah, a beautiful baby girl.

That was only the first of many surprises of motherhood for Dale.

In the first six months of Savannah's life, Dale experienced both the ecstatic highs and rock-bottom lows common to the adjustment of motherhood. She felt the wonder of indescribable love. The fatigue. The frustration of rarely finishing anything. The joy of watching her baby respond to the world.

On this day, she felt discouraged about the lack of accomplishment and time for herself. To exercise. Or read the Bible. Even to clean the house.

I listened.

"I used to feel the same way," I told her, "but I realize now that I was fanatic about picking up toys and cleaning off kitchen counters. I think I measured my significance by my ability to bring order to the chaos in our family room. It took me years to untangle myself from that habit and learn to relax my standards.

"Sometimes I think we should live our lives backward," I went on. "That way, we could use the wisdom we gain in our experiences to help us mellow out and enjoy the challenges along the way."

Before we hung up, Dale mentioned that she was getting together regularly with a new mother in her neighborhood. "She just had twins, and she needs some encouragment!" Dale explained.

Soon we said good-bye, promising to talk again soon.

Later, I thought about our conversation and marveled at its tidbits. Dale's discouragement. My encouragement. My recognition of what I'd learned as I looked back on my own experiences. Dale's enthusiasm for helping another new mother.

I realized I was all wrong about the benefits of living life backward.

God's plan is the opposite, of course, and it is really the best. He unfolds our days before us one at a time, which requires us to walk forward, maybe unsteadily at times. But we grow as we go and learn through our mistakes, and our uncertain steps help us to recognize our dependence upon God.

There's something else that happens in that plan: It gives us the opportunity to reach out and encourage those coming along behind us.

I once heard a statement that no matter where we are in life, we are always a window to the future for those behind us. By sharing our experiences, we can show them the way. We can reach around and extend a helping hand.

We tell our stories, especially the ones about discovering God's love for us and seeing his presence and the truth of his promises in our everyday moments.

These are the places we have left footprints of faith for others to follow. The lessons we have learned become stepping stones for others to follow.

In looking back, we discover yet another blessing: We see how far we've come and how God has faithfully drawn us closer to himself. It's as if God tells us, "Look back, my child, and see all that I have taught you." That look into life's rearview mirror helps us live more fully in the present, with greater trust that God is walking alongside us and has gone before us.

For me at mid-life, I need the trust and hope that comes from that reflective glace backward because I still have lots of questions about my future. Like how will I graciously cope with the issues of aging, such as growing forgetful or accepting the face I see in my new drivers license picture? How will I make the transition into new roles, like mother-in-law and grandmother? How will Lynn and I weather the Empty Nest season in our marriage?

I don't yet know the answers, but my experiences give me greater trust in God's promises. As he unfolds each day, I trust that he will provide what I need no matter what my circumstances ... and that he will weave today's difficulties together for tomorrow's blessings.

And no matter what happens today, I know I can trust his promise of hope: *The best is yet to come!*

A Record
of Footprints

At the end of each day, each year, each season of life, we look back at where we've been. We reflect upon the longings, transitions, obstacles, and temptations in our paths. We recognize those moments when life turned a corner and we came face to face with God. We recognize his nearness. His personal presence and involvement.

God tells us to remember those places:

> Only be careful, and watch yourselves closely so that you do not forget the things your eyes have seen or let them slip from your heart as long as you live. Teach them to your children and to their children after them (Deut. 4:9).

Moms are often the Remember-ers, the Keepers-of-Memories. We're also the Takers-of-Pictures, Makers-of-Scrapbooks, and Markers-of-Family-Milestones. For many of us, that instinct is knit deeply within our souls.

That's one reason I started keeping track of my own Footprints of Faith.

I wanted a record of God's faithfulness in my life, a visual aid to remind me of his constant presence. The practice is a biblical one. God directed his children to memorialize their experiences of his faithfulness. On the way to the Promised Land, he told the Israelites to save a jar of left-over manna, the bread he rained down from heaven to feed them (Ex. 16:33). He also told them to build a memorial of rocks on the banks of the Jordan River to remind them and their children of his protection in bringing them through the water.

In the same way, God wants us to remember his pattern of caring for us.

I started by remembering and writing down the defining moments or major milestones in my life—places where life seemed to stop or change direction: some childhood memories; my marriage; the birth of our first child; the death of my father....

Then I asked myself, as I looked back upon those milestones, what I learned about God in each of those places. Amazingly, I could see that God met me in each place, and I began to believe at least one of his promises in each experience. At each milestone, I took a step of growth in my faith.

As writer Richard Foster reflects in his book *Prayer*, "External events are springboards for understanding the deeper workings of God in the heart. We can turn back the pages of our personal history as often as we like and see the issues we have struggled with and the progress we have made."

How about recording some of your own Footprints of Faith?

Start by considering the milestones in your life. Below are some questions to get you thinking. As you attempt to answer them, ask what you learned about God in each situation. (You might check the Collection of Promises following this section.) If you have an answer, you have discovered one of your own Footprints of Faith.

1. What is one of the most difficult experiences you've ever faced in your life? What did you learn in that experience?
2. What is a time in which you really felt your mother's love? Your father's love?
3. What experience has helped you recognize what matters most in your life? The importance of priorities? The meaning of success?
4. What are your greatest temptations?
5. If you are married, what was your greatest adjustment to marriage?
6. If you are single, what is your greatest struggle?

7. If you have children, what was the most difficult challenge you faced in adjusting to motherhood?
8. Describe a personal experience in which God seemed real and near to you.

MY OWN FOOTPRINTS OF FAITH

Here is a sample of my Footprints of Faith:

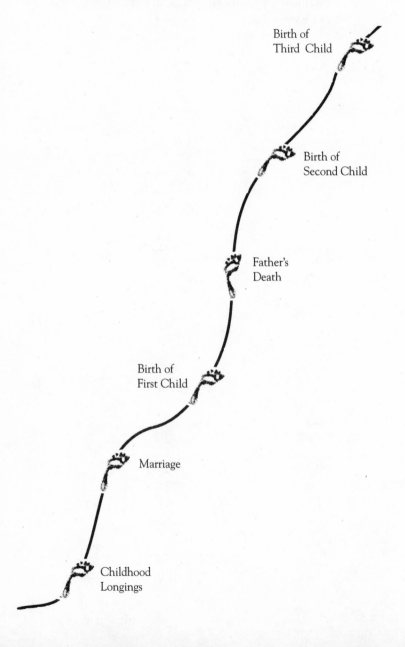

Birth of
Third Child

Birth of
Second Child

Father's
Death

Birth of
First Child

Marriage

Childhood
Longings

YOUR FOOTPRINTS OF FAITH

A Collection
of Promises

All of our lives, we search for truth. We seek to believe something that will never let us down. Something that never changes. Something that remains when all else fails, and that comes from someone who never fails us.

That Someone is God, and that something is his Word.

His promises are true. Always.

Every promise has been fulfilled; not one has failed (Josh. 23:14).

As I look back over my own life and seek to record my own footprints of faith, I see how I have grown and changed as I have learned, believed, and stood on God's promises.

So I end this book with this collection of God's promises.

God's promises are sprinkled throughout the pages of the Bible. They are statements of truth about what God will do for his children, because our faith enables us to understand the responses that help us experience the divine results.

In his book *Knowing God*, J. I. Packer describes a promise as "the proper God-given basis for all our life of faith" and suggests that the way to strengthen one's faith is to focus upon the particular promises that speaks to one's condition.

Knowing God's promises will equip you; believing them—and acting like you believe them—could change your life.

So I end this book with a collection of God's promises. As you read them, may you be like Abraham, who was "fully persuaded that God had power to do what he had promised" (Rom. 4:21).

Collection of Promises

(Note: all Scripture is from NIV unless otherwise indicated.)

When you feel all alone:

Do not fear, for I am with you; do not be dismayed, for I am your God. I will strengthen you and help you; I will uphold you with my righteous right hand.

Isaiah 41:10

When you are tired and discouraged:

I can do everything through him who gives me strength.

Philippians 4:13

When you need stability and security in an insecure place:

Jesus Christ is the same yesterday and today and forever.

Hebrews 13:8

When you doubt God's ability to handle your problems:

For nothing is impossible with God.

Luke 1:37

When you feel weighted down by worries and problems:

Cast your cares on the LORD and he will sustain you.

Psalm 55:22

When you need strength:

In quietness and trust is your strength . . .

Isaiah 30:15

The joy of the LORD is your strength.

Nehemiah 8:10

When you feel overwhelmed with too much to do:

Your strength will equal your days.

Deuteronomy 33:25

When you feel forgotten:

> *I will not forget you! See, I have engraved you on the palms of my hands.*
> Isaiah 49:15–16

When you wonder if God is enough:

> *And my God will meet all your needs according to his glorious riches in Christ Jesus.*
>
> Philippians 4:19

When God seems silent:

> *You will seek me and find me when you seek me with all your heart.*
> Jeremiah 29:13

When you need to know you are forgiven:

> *If we confess our sins, he is faithful and just and will forgive us our sins. . . .*
> 1 John 1:9

When you need assurance of God's nearness:

> *Never will I leave you; never will I forsake you.*
>
> Hebrews 13:5

> *I will be with you always, to the very end of the age.*
>
> Matthew 28:20

When you need assurance of God's love:

> *I have loved you with an everlasting love; I have drawn you with loving-kindness.*
>
> Jeremiah 31:3

> *Nothing—nothing living or dead, angelic or demonic, today or tomorrow, high or low, thinkable or unthinkable—absolutely nothing can get between us and God's love because of the way that Jesus our Master has embraced us.*
>
> Romans 8 (THE MESSAGE)

When you need assurance of your value and self-worth:

> *You knit me together in my mother's womb. I praise you because I am fearfully and wonderfully made.*
>
> Psalm 139:13–14

When you wonder about your purpose in life:

> *The LORD will fulfill his purpose for me.*
>
> Psalm 138:8

When you don't understand God:

*For my thoughts are not your thoughts, neither are your ways my ways. . . .
As the heavens are higher than the earth, so are my ways higher than your
ways and my thoughts than your thoughts.*

Isaiah 55:8–9

When you're struggling with your past:

Forget the former things; do not dwell on the past. See, I am doing a new thing!
Isaiah 43:18–19

When you need protection:

*Even though I walk through the valley of the shadow of death, I will fear
no evil, for you are with me; your rod and your staff, they comfort me.*
Psalm 23:4

When you are in trouble:

God is our refuge and strength, an ever present help in trouble.
Psalm 46:1

When you are hurting and don't understand why:

*For I know the plans I have for you . . . plans to prosper you and not to
harm you, plans to give you a hope and a future.*
Jeremiah 29:11

*We also rejoice in our sufferings, because we know that suffering pro-
duces perseverance; perseverance, character; and character, hope. And
hope does not disappoint us . . .*

Romans 5:3–4

When you need hope in suffering:

In this world you will have trouble. But take heart! I have overcome the world.
John 16:33

*And the God of all grace . . . , after you have suffered a little while, will
himself restore you and make you strong, firm and steadfast.*
1 Peter 5:10

When you need confidence in your ability to cope:

*For God did not give us a spirit of timidity, but a spirit of power, of love
and of self-discipline.*

2 Timothy 1:7

When you are waiting:

Those who hope in the LORD will renew their strength. They will soar on wings like eagles; they will run and not grow weary, they will walk and not be faint.

Isaiah 40:31

When, as a mother, you need to know God cares:

He tends his flock like a shepherd: He gathers the lambs in his arms and carries them close to his heart; he gently leads those that have young.

Isaiah 40:11

When the drudgery of everyday tasks gets you down, and you need to know that mothering matters:

Be shepherds of God's flock that is under your care, serving as overseers— not because you must, but because you are willing. . . . And when the Chief Shepherd appears, you will receive the crown of glory that will never fade away.

1 Peter 5: 2, 4

. . . he who humbles himself will be exalted.

Luke 18:14

When you need God's direction:

Whether you turn to the right or to the left, your ears will hear a voice behind you saying, "This is the way; walk in it."

Isaiah 30:21

When you feel unable to love another:

We love because he first loved us.

1 John 4:19

When you need to know God hears your prayers:

You will pray to him, and he will hear you . . .

Job 22:27

. . . if we ask anything according to his will, he hears us.

1 John 5:14

When you need to know the importance of the Bible:

The grass withers and the flowers fall, but the word of the Lord stands forever.

1 Peter 1:24–25

Then you will know the truth, and the truth will set you free.

John 8:32

For the word of God is living and active. Sharper than any double-edged sword . . . it judges the thoughts and attitudes of the heart.

Hebrews 4:12

When you wonder what faith is:

Now faith is being sure of what we hope for and certain of what we do not see.

Hebrews 11:1

When you wonder if you can believe God:

What I have said, that will I bring about; what I have planned, that will I do.

Isaiah 46:11

When you need assurance of your faith:

For God so loved the world that he gave his one and only Son, that whoever believes in him shall not perish but have eternal life.

John 3:16

If you confess with your mouth, "Jesus is Lord," and believe in your heart that God raised him from the dead, you will be saved.

Romans 10:9

I tell you the truth, he who believes has everlasting life.

John 6:47

When you need hope for your future:

No eye has seen, no ear has heard, no mind has conceived what God has prepared for those who love him.

1 Corinthians 2:9

The MOPS Story

MOPS stands for Mothers of Preschoolers, a program designed for mothers with children under school age. From its humble beginnings in a church in Wheat Ridge, Colorado, MOPS International now charters MOPS groups in more than 1,200 churches and parachurch organizations in all fifty States and in twelve other countries.

Some fifty thousand moms are touched by their local MOPS groups, and many, many more are encouraged through *Mom Sense* radio broadcast and newsletter and publications such as this book. MOPS groups meet the unique needs of mothers of preschoolers in a variety of settings, including urban, suburban, rural, and Teen MOPS. Mission MOPS provides funds for organizations which need financial assistance for MOPS group leadership training and chartering.

MOPS grew out of a desire to meet the needs of every mother of preschoolers. Today, when a mom enters a MOPS meeting, she is greeted by a friendly face and escorted to MOPPETS, where her children enjoy their special part of the MOPS program. In MOPPETS, children from infancy through kindergarten experience a caring environment while they learn, sing, play, and make crafts.

Once her children are settled, the MOPS mom joins a program tailor-made to meet her needs. She can grab something good to eat and not have to share it! She can finish a sentence and not have to speak in Children-ese!

The program typically begins with a brief lesson taught by an older mom who's been through the challenging early years of mothering and who can share from her experience and from the truths taught in the Bible. Then the women move into small discussion groups where each mom is free to share her joys and struggles with other moms who truly understand her feelings.

After this, the women participate in a craft or other creative activity. For moms who are often frustrated by the impossibility of completing anything in their unpredictable days, this time is deeply satisfying. It provides a sense of accomplishment and growth for many moms.

Because mothers of preschoolers themselves lead MOPS, the program also offers women a chance to develop their leadership skills and other talents. It takes organizational skills, financial management, and creativity to run a MOPS program successfully.

To find out if there is a MOPS group near you, or if you're interested in learning how to start a MOPS group in your community, please write or call the MOPS International office:

MOPS International
P.O. Box 102200
Denver, CO 80250-2200
Phone: (303) 733-5353
       800-929-1287
Fax: (303) 733-5770
E-mail: Info @MOPS.org

REMEMBER TO LOOK FOR THESE OTHER GREAT BOOKS FROM MOPS

Mom's Devotional Bible

Moms, you don't have to go it alone! The *Mom's Devotional Bible* is a companion and trusted source of wisdom to help you along the path of mothering. A full year of weekday devotions written by Elisa Morgan, president of MOPS (Mothers of Preschoolers) International, are combined with the Bible text to offer you and moms everywhere fresh perspective on topics such as time management, mentors for moms, sibling rivalry, and much more. And on weekends, find new insight as you explore "special interest" areas like "A Mother's Legacy," "Train Up a Child," "A Time to Play," and "Get Growing!"

The complete text of the best-selling New International Version provides accuracy you can trust. A list of resources in the back of the Bible shows you where to turn for help with the special challenges you face as a mother. And from family traditions to praying for young children, twenty full-color pages add a warm, keepsake touch. The *Mom's Devotional Bible*—get yours today!

Hardcover: 0-310- 92501-0
Softcover: 0-310-92422-7

A wide selection of *Mom's Devotional Bible* gift products are also available.

What Every Mom Needs

Being the mother of a young child is a tough job, but now you can find help and understanding. Elisa Morgan and Carol Kuykendall of MOPS point the way to relief and fulfillment in the midst of motherhood's hectic pace. In *What Every Mom Needs*, Elisa and Carol identify your nine basic needs—significance, identity, growth, intimacy, instruction, help, recreation, perspective, and hope—and show you how meeting those needs will make you more content, and a better mom at the same time.

Softcover: 0-310-20097-0
Also available in audio pages, 0-310-20417-8

COMING IN AUGUST 1997 . . .

What Every Child Needs

Elisa Morgan and Carol Kuykendall come together again! This time Elisa and Carol detail in a warm and nurturing style the nine needs of every child: security, affirmation, family, respect, play, guidance, discipline, independence, and hope. Don't miss the great stories, helpful hints and practical suggestions that will help you recognize and meet these needs in the life of your child.

Softcover: 0-310-21151-4
Also available in audio pages, 0-310-21579-X

Learning to Let Go

Helping our children to become independent adults is a parenting challenge that is often overlooked. But in *Learning to Let Go*, Carol Kuykendall explains that letting go is one of the most important jobs a parent is blessed to have. Join Carol as she defines what "letting go" really is, its biblical basis, how it happens, and—best of all—its great rewards.

Softcover: 0-310-33621-X

We want to hear from you. Please send your comments about this
book to us in care of the address below. Thank you.

ZondervanPublishingHouse
Grand Rapids, Michigan 49530
http://www.zondervan.com